PERENNIALS

1001 Gardening Questions Answered

by
The Editors of Garden Way Publishing

Foreword by Lewis and Nancy Hill

STOREY

Storey Communications, Inc.
Pownal, Vermont 05261

Produced by Storey Communications, Inc.
President, M. John Storey
Executive Vice President of Administration, Martha M. Storey
Executive Vice President of Operations, Douglas B. Rhodes
Publisher, Thomas Woll

Written by Maggie Oster and the Editors of Garden Way Publishing
Interior design by Andrea Gray
Edited by Gwen W. Steege
Production by Andrea Gray and Rebecca Babbitt
Front cover photograph by Derek Fell
Back cover photograph by Maggie Oster
Interior photographs by Madelaine Gray, Cindy McFarland, Maggie
Oster, Positive Images (Margaret Hensel), and Ann Reilly
Chapter opening photographs by Madelaine Gray (1), Maggie Oster
(2, 4, 5), Positive Images (Margaret Hensel) (3)
Map by Northern Cartographic
Typesetting by The Best Type and Design on Earth, Burlington, VT

Copyright © 1989 by Doubleday Book & Music Clubs, Inc.

Library of Congress Catalog Card Number: 88-82824
International Standard Book Number: 0-88266-548-0

Library of Congress Cataloging in Publication Data

Perennials: 1001 gardening questions answered.

Bibliography: p.
Includes index.
1. Perennials—Miscellanea. I. Garden Way Publishing.
SB434.P4735 1989   635.9′32   88-82824
ISBN 0-88266-548-0

Contents

Like most gardeners, we find that the more we know about growing plants, the more we enjoy the process of cultivating them. It's always much more fun to plant and care for a garden when we meet with success—when each plant flourishes and the garden design looks like a well-planned tapestry, rather than a hodgepodge. Yet those of us who grow things, experts and novices alike, always have many un-answered questions, and *Perennials: 1001 Gardening Questions Answered* rises to the challenge. Here is a wealth of information about over one hundred herbaceous perennials, with their extremely varied sizes, shapes, colors, growing habits, blooming times, hardiness, prefer-ences for certain soil types and sun and shade conditions, and disease susceptibilities.

"When do I divide my plants?" "Should I cut back tall growing perennials in the fall?" "What are the best perennials for a low-maintenance garden?" These are three of the innumerable questions that are answered clearly and completely in this volume. Many are the classic questions that every gardener has asked at some stage of growing perennials; others furnish helpful answers and fascinating facts about things we wouldn't even have thought of asking —but are glad someone did.

Whatever your skills or interests, you will have fun browsing through this book for new ideas and encouragement. The arrange-ment of color, one of the most difficult challenges in planning a perennial garden, is explained with the easiest-to-follow directions we have ever seen. The fine list of perennials recommended for various types of plantings — from bird and butterfly gardens to shade and woodland areas —includes many excellent species too often neglected. If you have trouble finding the plants you want at your local garden center, the list of mail-order nurseries in the Appendix will help you locate all the plants recommended in the book.

Just as avid cooks enjoy browsing through the recipes in a good cookbook, both beginning and experienced gardeners will often turn to *Perennials: 1001 Gardening Questions Answered*. Of course, we nursery people may find ourselves being asked fewer and fewer questions on the subject — a state of affairs not particularly to our liking, for all gardeners, including us, welcome any excuse to talk about our favorite subject, plants. For gardeners constantly looking for a source of information and inspiration, however, this is a book that will not be relegated to the top shelves of the garden library, but left handy for frequent reading and reference.

Lewis and Nancy Hill

Richard Brown

1 *Planning the Perennial Garden*

For the gardener who enjoys combining colors and textures to weave living tapestry, there is no better group of plants to work with than perennials. Favorite perennials—such as chrysanthemum, daylily, iris, and peony—which by definition, bloom in one season, die back in the winter, and then renew from the same roots each spring for at least several years, offer varying degrees of challenge and limitless possibilities. Their cost is reasonable, and results are fairly soon achieved. Garden designs can be changed frequently and relatively easily. Unlike the 100-foot long, eight- to ten-foot-wide perennial borders of the past, today's perennial gardens are greatly simplified, so care is minimal, yet the impact on the landscape is still maximized. For the smallest garden, where just a few species are used for accent, to the most ambitious, where massed plantings display dozens of varieties, perennials offer longevity as well as a beauty that is hard to achieve with annuals, shrubs, or bulbs alone.

ASSESSING YOUR SITE

Before trying to plan and plant perennials, you must first consider the growing environment that is available in your region and in your yard. The key factors are soil, moisture, light, and temperature. To garden successfully, you must have an understanding of the basics of each of these factors and their role in plant growth. To some extent, these factors can be modified,

◀ *Weave a living tapestry with the massed colors and textures of perennial flowers such as chrysanthemums.*

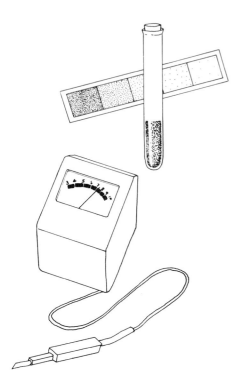

Determine the nutrient content and pH levels of your soil by testing your soil with readily available testing kits.

but it makes sense to make the most of what you have and to select plants that will readily adapt to what is already there. Ways to modify each of the factors will be discussed in Chapter 3, "Planting and Caring for Perennials." First, let's take a look at the role of each of these factors and at which plants adapt best to various conditions.

Soil

How do I find out what kind of soil I have?

The simplest, most precise way is to have your soil tested by a commercial soil-testing laboratory or by the Cooperative Extension Service in your county. This agency is the educational arm of the U.S. Department of Agriculture. There is a branch in every county in the country, often affiliated with the State University. For information on taking the samples and where to send them, call your county's Cooperative Extension Service office. The results should tell you the type of soil you have, such as sandy or clay loam, the pH, and the status of the major nutrients, or levels of nitrogen, phosphorus, and potassium.

What type of soil do most perennials need?

Most perennials grow best in humus-rich soil that has a relatively even balance of clay, sand, and silt particles. This "perfect" soil is called loam. It will hold moisture for a reasonable length of time, yet drains quickly enough so that it does not remain soggy for very long after rain or watering.

What nutrient elements are essential for perennials?

The three elements essential to plant growth are nitrogen, phosphorus, and potassium, often referred to by their chemical symbols, N,P,K.

Nitrogen is part of the structure of protoplasm, chlorophyll, and various plant foods, and is needed for both the vegetative and reproductive stages of growth. *Phosphorus* is essential to cell division and for the formation of nucleoproteins; it aids root development, hastens maturity, stiffens tissues, and stimulates flower and seed production. *Potassium* (in the form of potash) is necessary for the manufacture and movement of starches and sugar; it is a general conditioner, overcoming succulence and brittleness, hastening maturity and seed production, and aiding in root development.

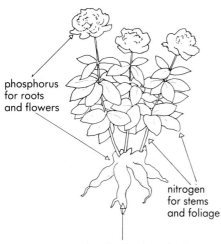

phosphorus for roots and flowers

nitrogen for stems and foliage

potassium for food production

Balanced garden fertilizers provide nitrogen (N) for foliage and stem growth, phosphorus (P) for root development and flower production, and potassium (K) for plant metabolism and food production.

In layman's terms, what do each of the nutrients do for perennials?

Nitrogen is necessary for foliage and stem growth and for dark green leaf color. Phosphorus is necessary for root development and flower production. Potassium is necessary for plant metabolism and the production of food. For perennials, it is important that the second element, phosphorus, be higher than or equal to nitrogen. If it is not, you will have a lot of growth but few flowers.

What are trace elements?

Trace elements such as boron, chlorine, copper, iron, magnesium, manganese, molybdenum, and zinc are present in most soils and are needed in very small amounts for plant nutrition. When decaying organic matter is used freely and when pH is held between 6.0 and 6.9, you can be fairly certain these elements will be present.

What perennials tolerate relatively infertile soils?

The same plants that are tolerant of light, sandy soils listed below.

What is humus?

For practical purposes, humus may be defined as the resultant brown substance that develops following the breakdown of organic materials by various soil organisms.

In what forms is potential humus available to the average home gardener?

Well-rotted manure, peat moss, decomposed kitchen waste, seaweed, sawdust, wood chips, pine needles, leaf mold, straw, or hay. The compost pile is probably the best of all sources of humus for the home gardener, but look around your area—there may be more possibilities than you realize.

Maggie Oster

Yucca and Autumn Joy stonecrop are two easy-to-grow perennials that tolerate light, sandy soils.

PERENNIALS THAT TOLERATE LIGHT, SANDY SOILS

baby's-breath	globe thistle	sea holly
basket-of-gold	golden marguerite	spider wort
blackberry lily	goldenrod	spurge
blanket flower	hardy aster	sundrops
blue stars	hardy pinks	sunrose
butterfly flower	hen-and-chickens	stonecrop
candytuft	hollyhock mallow	thrift
Carolina lupine	lamb's ears	tickseed
catmint	Maltese cross	torch lily
coneflower	purple rockcress	wormwood
daylily	Russian sage	yarrow
false indigo	sage	yucca
gay-feather		

PERENNIALS THAT TOLERATE HEAVY, CLAY SOILS

bear's-breech	Greek valerian	ragwort
bee balm	hardy aster	saxifrage
bugleweed	lady's-mantle	self-heal
coneflower	leopard's-bane	sneezeweed
daylily	loosestrife	Solomon's-seal
foxglove	meadow rue	spotted dead nettle
goatsbeard	mist flower	windflower
goldenrod	purple loosestrife	

What is the function of humus in the soil?

Humus affects granulation of the soil, thereby improving drainage and soil aeration; increases the soil's water-holding capacity; increases bacterial activity in the soil; increases the percentage of such essential elements as nitrogen and sulfur; and helps to make nonavailable, essential elements available to plants.

What is pH?

The term pH refers to the measurement of the concentration of the hydrogen ion in a given substance on a scale from 0 to 14. The midpoint, or pH 7, is considered neutral, while those numbers less than seven are considered in the range of acidity and the numbers above seven in the range of alkalinity. The small pH test kits sold in garden centers are adequate and usually give a reading within a tenth of a point or so.

Why is pH important?

First, certain nutrients can be absorbed by plants only within specific pH ranges. Second, the activity of soil microorganisms is affected by pH, ceasing entirely at pH 4.0 and below. Another effect of pH is the release of toxic elements, such as aluminum, at both a low pH and a high pH value. The prevalence of certain diseases is also affected by pH.

What pH is best for most plants?

The point at which all elements are available to plants except those that require highly acid soil is pH 6.5. At neutral (7.0), acidity and alkalinity balance each other out. Thus, somewhere between 6.0 and 7.0 is perhaps the best point to strive for when you alter soil acidity.

Windflower may be grown in heavy, clay soils.

What are some perennials that grow well on acid soils of fair to good fertility (pH 5.0 to 5.5)?

Butterfly flower, gentian, *Iris ensata,* lupine, Virginia blue-bells, primrose, and violet.

What are some perennials that do not grow well on strongly acid soils, but prefer slightly acid to neutral soils (pH 6.5 to 7.0)?

Baby's-breath, basket-of-gold, bear's-breech, bellflower, be-tony, blue plumbago, campion, candytuft, catmint, chrysanthe-mum, cupid's-dart, daylily, delphinium, desert-candle, flax, foxglove, gas plant, globe thistle, golden marguerite, hardy aster, hardy pinks, hen-and-chickens, iris, lavender cotton, lobelia, Oriental poppy, ornamental onion, pearly everlasting, perennial cornflower, perennial sunflower, perennial sweet pea, phlox, purple rockcress, red valerian, Russian sage, sage, saxifrage, sea holly, snow-in-summer, stonecrop, sunrose, thrift, tickseed, toadflax, torch lily, yarrow.

Moisture

What is the role of water in plant growth?

Water is vital to healthy growth, as plants are ninety percent water; water is also necessary for absorption of nutrients.

Why is excess water a problem?

Roots are incapable of absorbing water and nutrients unless oxygen is also present in the soil. A plant top can actually wilt for lack of water while its roots are completely submerged. The ideal soil is one that can absorb abundant water in its organic substances, but also one in which the passages between the organic and mineral particles are filled with air.

Will you explain the terms "well-drained soil" and "waterlogged soil"?

A well-drained soil is one in which surplus water runs off quickly and which dries out readily after a rain or watering. A waterlogged soil is the opposite, containing too much water and little air. Soil can become waterlogged if it contains too much peat moss.

Stonecrops are among the plants that tolerate drought conditions.

Ann Reilly

Why would a loose, crumbly loam stay soggy?

Possibly there is a problem with drainage beneath the topsoil, in the subsoil layer. This can be corrected by having drainage tiles installed or by constructing raised beds.

What are some perennials that tolerate drought conditions?

Baby's-breath, basket-of-gold, bishop's hat, blanket flower, bleeding-heart, butterfly flower, campion, candytuft, catmint, foxglove, gayfeather, golden marguerite, hardy aster, hen-and-chickens, hollyhock mallow, lamb's ears, lily-of-the-valley, lily-turf, purple rockcress, rue, Russian sage, saxifrage, sea holly, Solomon's-seal, spotted dead nettle, spurge, stonecrop, sundrops, sunrose, tickseed, thrift, yarrow, yucca.

What are some perennials that tolerate wet soils?

Astilbe, avens, bee balm, daylily, forget-me-not, globeflower, goatsbeard, hardy aster, *Iris ensata,* lobelia, loosestrife, marsh marigold, plantain lily, primrose, purple loosestrife, queen-of-the-prairie, rose mallow, Siberian iris, snake grass, Virginia bluebells.

Light

How much sunlight do most perennials need?

Most common perennials do best in full sunlight, but there are many that can get by quite well if they receive only a half day of full sun. The shady period of the day should come from a vertical surface, such as a wall, hedge, or building, rather than from a tree, which offers root competition as well as shade.

How does exposure to sun affect blooming?

In various ways, depending on characteristics unique to certain plants. For example, a plant like chrysanthemum may bloom earlier if grown with afternoon shade because diminishing light conditions trigger its flowering mechanism. Conversely, other plants, such as peonies, grown with afternoon shade may bloom later in spring. Also, some flower colors, like the red or pink blooms of daylilies, are "washed out" in bright light.

Do light requirements differ for gardens farther north?

Most definitely. A plant that needs a location with full sun in the north may need light shade in order to grow well in southern climates. This is due both to the intensity of the light as well as to temperature. Also, midsummer days in the south are shorter than those in the north. Because they receive more light in the north, plants grow more quickly there.

What are some perennials that grow in the heaviest shade?

Bishop's hat, bleeding-heart, bugleweed, Christmas rose, foxglove, lily-of-the-valley, lily-turf, plantain lily, saxifrage, Siberian bugloss, Solomon's-seal, spotted dead nettle, violet.

What are some perennials that tolerate light shade?

Astilbe, bear's-breech, bee balm, bellflower, blue plumbago, bugbane, columbine, coralbells, creeping phlox, daylily, globeflower, goatsbeard, lady's-mantle, leopard's-bane, lobelia, loosestrife, lungwort, meadow rue, meadowsweet, primrose, Siberian iris, spurge, Virginia bluebells, windflower.

Temperature

What are hardiness zones?

The United States Department of Agriculture classifies regions of the country according to annual minimum temperatures and/or the length of growing seasons. These range from the near-tundra Zone 1 to the subtropical Zone 10, which seldom has frost. Rather than listing the hardiness zones with the plants in this book, the minimum winter temperature is given instead.

Do summer temperatures also affect plant growth and flowering?

Most definitely. Gardeners in the south face heat, humidity, and drought in the summer. In those conditions, plants may require frequent watering and light shade, as well as humus-rich

Lupine, pink and red yarrow, and purple loosestrife all grow well in regions as far south as those with minimum winter temperatures of only 20° F.

Maggie Oster

soils and a summer mulch to help them stay cooler. Windbreaks give valuable protection from hot, drying winds. Plants may go dormant in August, but then have a long fall season.

What are some perennials that grow best in areas that have cool summers?

Astilbe, beard-tongue, bleeding-heart, Christmas rose, columbine, delphinium, ferns, lupine, meadow rue, and primrose.

What are some perennials that will grow well as far south as areas with a minimum winter temperature of 20° F.?

Avens, balloon flower, beard-tongue, bear's-breech, bee balm, bellflower, blanket flower, bleeding-heart, blue plumbago, blue stars, bugbane, butterfly flower, campion, chrysanthemum, coneflower, coralbells, daylily, false indigo, foxglove, gay-feather, globe thistle, goatsbeard, golden marguerite, goldenrod, iris, lamb's-ears, meadowsweet, phlox, pincushion flower, plantain lily, purple coneflower, purple loosestrife, orange sunflower, ornamental grasses, rose mallow, sage, saxifrage, Siberian bugloss, snake grass, speedwell, spurge, Stokes' aster, stonecrop, sunrose, thrift, tickseed, torch lily, Virginia bluebells, wormwood, yarrow.

Why would a plant, supposedly hardy in a certain region, not live through winter?

There are several reasons, and soil temperature, rather than air temperature, is the more critical factor. Hardy perennials may die if there is no insulating snow cover or if alternate periods of freezing and thawing occur, causing plants to be heaved out of the ground. This can often be prevented by using a winter mulch.

What kinds of materials are good for mulching perennials in the winter?

Place leaves, straw, or wood chips around the plants, but not up against the crown (the point where stem and roots merge), to help to protect the roots. Place evergreen boughs over the crown of the plant.

When mulching with leaves or straw, leave a space around the crown of the plant, then cover the plant lightly with evergreen boughs.

Do late-blooming perennials present special problems?

Yes, because even if a plant is winter hardy, some, such as asters, chrysanthemums, gentians, rose mallow, and windflowers, may not bloom before the first autumn frosts.

What are some perennials that are the most tolerant of severe winter temperatures (-30° F. or below)?

Baby's-breath, balloon flower, basket-of-gold, bellflower (some species), blanket flower, bleeding-heart, blue stars, bugbane, bugleweed, bugloss, butterfly flower, Carolina lupine, catmint, coneflower, coralbells, gas plant, gay-feather, globe thistle, goatsbeard, golden marguerite, Greek valerian, leopard's-bane, lobelia, lungwort, mallow, Maltese cross, meadowsweet, mist flower, monkshood, Oriental poppy, ornamental onion, painted daisy, pearly everlasting, peony, perennial cornflower, phlox, pincushion flower, plantain lily, plume poppy, purple coneflower, purple loosestrife, Siberian iris, sneezeweed, snow-on-the-mountain, speedwell, stonecrop, tickseed, turtlehead, Virginia bluebells, wormwood, yarrow.

CONSIDERING THE PLANTS' CHARACTERISTICS

Once you have assessed your site for the factors of soil, moisture, light, and temperature, the next step is to consider the plants themselves. This, too, has several aspects, including height, bloom season, color, shape, texture, and growth habit (how much the plant spreads).

Height and Season of Bloom

How do I arrange plants in a new perennial border?

Essentially, you should think of a flower border as a group photo. The taller plants go in the back, midsize ones toward the center, and the shorter plants in the front, or foreground. In an island bed, the taller plants are toward the center, with medium and short plants on either side. However, for flower beds and borders to appear most natural and pleasing, there should be some overlap among the various heights.

Are there other factors with regard to height that I should think about?

Yes, consider that some perennials are cut back after flowering; so, a plant that is tall in bloom, such as delphinium, may be much shorter when the faded flowers are removed. Or, conversely, for most of the summer, plantain lilies are low, rounded plants, but in late summer they send up spikes of flowers. Complicating this whole process are the facts that some cultivars of one species grow taller than other cultivars of the same species and that mature height depends greatly on soil, light, moisture, and climate. (A *species* is the fundamental classification, including individuals that resemble one another and can breed together, but not usually with plants of other species. *Cultivars*—cultivated varieties, sometimes called varieties—are subdivisions of the species that have been bred together and maintain their characteristics under continued cultivation.)

The sequence of bloom is another major factor in the design of a perennial garden. Many gardeners like to design their flower gardens to have blossoms from early spring until fall frosts. This

Plan your flower beds so that tall plants are in the back, midsize ones toward the center, and short plants in the front, with some overlap among the various heights for the most pleasing effect.

Periods of Bloom and Relative Heights
of Selected Perennials

TALL (4 feet or more)	MEDIUM (1-4 feet)	SHORT (1 foot or less)

SPRING

columbine	catmint	basket-of-gold
dame's-rocket	cranesbill	bleeding-heart
globeflower	early daylily	*(Dicentra exima)*
Japanese bleeding-heart	flax	candytuft
leopard's-bane	sweet William	creeping phlox
Maltese-cross	Virginia bluebells	dwarf iris
mountain bluet		primrose
painted daisy		purple rockcress
Siberian iris		rock cress
sneezeweed		violet
spurge		

EARLY SUMMER

Carolina lupine	astilbe	Carpathian harebell
daylily	avens	coralbells
delphinium	beard-tongue	
false indigo	bellflower	
foxglove	butterfly flower	
gas plant	cranesbill	
German iris	daylily	
globe thistle	golden marguerite	
lupine	Oriental poppy	
mallow	painted daisy	
peony	perennial cornflower	
	speedwell	

MID- TO LATE SUMMER

baby's-breath	astilbe	flax
bee balm	balloon flower	lamb's ears
bugbane	blanket flower	sea lavender
daylily	campion	Stokes' aster
false starwort	coneflower	
gay-feather	globe thistle	
monkshood	phlox	
phlox	plantain lily	
purple loosestrife	shasta daisy	
rose mallow	torch lily	
sneezeweed	turtlehead	

LATE SUMMER AND FALL

bugbane	blanket flower	dwarf aster
false starwort	blue plumbago	dwarf chrysanthemum
hardy aster	chrysanthemum	dwarf stonecrop
lobelia	coneflower	
mist flower	mist flower	
monkshood	sage	
perennial sunflower	speedwell	
phlox	stonecrop	
rose mallow	turtlehead	
sneezeweed		
windflower		

is easier said than done, for plants and weather do not always cooperate. Still, it is possible to plan a garden around the approximate blooming period.

How can I organize the information about the plants that I want to grow in my own garden?

A perennial garden is continually evolving. Keep a notebook for recording blooming times, plant heights, and combinations that you observe in your area and garden. Then, you can move plants around in the garden, creating an ever more pleasurable garden.

Can you list some reliable perennials by the period of bloom and relative heights?

One can give only approximate ranges, because some plants bloom for long periods, spanning the seasons, and some have low, medium, or tall cultivars within the species. Also, what is tall in the spring may be medium the rest of the year. Refer to the chart on page 11 for guidance in planning the season of bloom and the height of the perennials you would like to grow.

Periods of Bloom of Selected Perennials

MARCH-APRIL	MAY	AUGUST-SEPTEMBER
basket-of-gold	basket-of-gold	balloon flower
bleeding-heart	bugleweed	bee balm
candytuft	cranesbill	blanket flower
catmint	dame's-rocket	bugbane
Christmas rose	flax	chrysanthemum
creeping phlox	globeflower	coneflower
iris	Greek valerian	false dragonhead
marsh marigold	hardy pinks	false starwort
mountain bluet	leopard's-bane	flax
primrose	lupin	gay-feather
purple rockcress	mallow	golden marguerite
rock cress	Maltese-cross	hardy aster
spurge	painted daisy	lobelia
sweet william	peony	mist flower
violet	primrose	orange sunflower
Virginia bluebells	sneezeweed	perennial sunflower
	snow-in-summer	perennial sweet pea
	speedwell	phlox
	stonecrop	pincushion flower
	thrift	plantain lily
		plume poppy
		purple coneflower
		rose mallow
		sage
		sneezeweed
		speedwell
		Stokes' aster
		stonecrop
		turtlehead
		windflower

My garden looks really wonderful during June and July, but is not very interesting in spring or fall. What do you suggest for those times of the year?

Although blooming time varies in different parts of the country, the times listed in the chart on page 12 are appropriate for much of those parts of the country with minimum winter temperatures of -10 to -20° F.

Color

Color in the garden has the same effect on feelings and moods as it does in your home or clothing. A vibrant color like red makes a flower bed seem larger and closer, while blues will make it appear smaller and more distant. The quantity and combinations of color used, as well as lighting, also affect our perceptions.

One of the greatest challenges of growing perennials is combining them not only according to height and period of bloom but also with regard to harmonious use of color.

The perennial borders I've tried before looked "blotchy." What was wrong?

Color makes a greater impact than any other aspect of garden design. If you mix many different colored flowers together, rather than carefully choose a color scheme, you will almost surely have the blotchy result you describe.

Is there some limit to the number of different colors I should use in a flower border?

The trend today, particularly in smaller gardens, is to choose one primary color, then add only about two more colors to the design.

What criteria should I use in choosing a color scheme?

It depends on your personal preferences, the color of your home, the climate, and the look you want to achieve. Reds, yellows, and oranges are warm colors, creating a feeling of activity, happiness, and cheerfulness. Cool tones—blues, purples, and pinks—are more relaxing.

Once I have chosen the main color I want to use, how do I select the others?

Using a color wheel, you can choose from several different color harmonies, or combinations. For example, if you select blue as your primary color, then orange is directly across the wheel from it. This is called *complementary* harmony. Another complementary harmony is yellow with purple. This is a strong combination and may be too overpowering in a small garden.

Pink combines well with purple and red-violet for an analogous color harmony.

Positive Images, Margaret Hensel

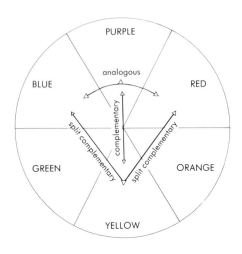

Use a color wheel to guide your choice of various color harmonies.

If you choose a primary color, say blue again, and work with one of the colors on either side of its opposite, this is called *split complementary harmony*. Examples of this are blue with yellow, or blue with red. You can also create complementary harmony using the intermediate colors, such as orange with violet.

A third type of harmony is *analogous harmony*, in which three colors in a row on the color wheel are used. Some examples of this are yellow-orange, orange, and red-orange, or blue-violet, blue, and blue-green.

What is monochromatic harmony?

A monochromatic harmony consists of only one color, such as all orange, all yellow, all pink, all blue. This can be monotonous unless you use different shades of the same color, as well as a wide variety of plants with a full range of heights and textures.

What about pink; where does it fit in?

Pink is actually a tone of red; mix red and white paint together and you have pink. In flower gardens, pink is often best combined with red-violet, violet, and blue flowers.

I like so many different kinds of flowers. Is there any way to combine many colors?

One way is to plant a border so that the colors flow along the color wheel. For example, start at one end with blue, purple, and red-violet flowers, then use pale shades of blue, followed by pale yellows, bright yellows, oranges, and end with red. The key to the success of this scheme is separating the primary colors with paler shades of the same color or with white flowers.

I have tried planting white flowers between colors but have not been satisfied. What makes it work?

You must plant a large enough area of white flowers in order to break up the colors.

Do I have to use the same color scheme in the back and sides of the garden that I've used in front?

No, you can use a different color scheme in each part of your yard. However, those areas that are relatively close together should be harmonious.

We have built a wonderful gazebo for our garden. What color flowers should we plant around it?

A focal point in the garden, such as a gazebo, should have bright flowers around it to draw the eye immediately to the brilliant reds, oranges, and yellows. If, on the other hand, you want to minimize an object in the garden, choose pastels, blues, and lavenders.

Is there some way to make my large property seem smaller?

Although there are ways in terms of overall design, such as dividing the property into smaller, roomlike areas, the colors you choose will also affect how large the space feels. For example, using the warmer tones of red, maroon, gold, orange, and yellow will make a garden look smaller than it is. Choosing plants with dark-colored foliage will also help.

Some favorite yellow perennials are basket-of-gold, Carolina lupine, cinquefoil, golden marguerite, goldenrod, leopard's-bane, orange and perennial sunflowers, sneezeweed, spurge, sundrops, tickseed, and yarrow. Red to orange standbys are avens, blackberry lily, blanket flower, butterfly flower, Maltese cross, Oriental poppy, and torch lily.

My townhouse garden is so small. Is there any way to make it look more expansive?

Choose colors that recede and calm, such as blue, lavender, purple, and white.

Some Examples of Color Harmonies

COMPLEMENTARY HARMONIES

YELLOW	WITH	PURPLE
basket-of-gold		bellflower
Carolina lupine		catmint
daylily		delphinium
goldenrod		false indigo
leopard's-bane		hardy aster
sundrops		iris
tickseed		monkshood
yarrow		sage
		speedwell

SPLIT COMPLEMENTARY HARMONIES

ORANGE	WITH	PURPLE
avens		bellflower
blackberry lily		catmint
butterfly flower		delphinium
Maltese-cross		false indigo
Oriental poppy		hardy aster
		iris
		monkshood
		sage
		speedwell

ANALOGOUS HARMONIES

YELLOW	WITH	ORANGE AND RED
daylily		avens
golden marguerite		blackberry lily
leopard's-bane		blanket flower
tickseed		butterfly flower
yarrow		Canadian columbine
		cardinal flower
		Oriental poppy
		torch lily

What are some easily grown blue-flowered perennials?

Speedwell (*Veronica* Crater Lake Blue, *V. longifolia subsessilis*), globe thistle, snake grass (*Tradescantia* James C. Weguelin), balloon flower (*Platycodon grandiflorus*), bellflower (*Campanula persicifolia*), blue plumbago, and blue stars.

Can you recommend some white flowers?

White windflower, rock cress, goatsbeard, false starwort, Shasta daisy, bugbane, gas plant, candytuft, gooseneck loosestrife, mallow (Alba), peony (Festiva Maxima), Oriental poppy (Field Marshall Vander Glotz), phlox (Miss Lingard and Mt. Fuji), and false dragonhead (Summer Snow).

I work at an office during the day and enjoy relaxing in the garden when I come home. What flowers look best at night?

White flowers as well as plants with silver or gray foliage show up very well at night. Some perennials to consider for their pale foliage include the various artemisias, rue, lavender cotton, Russian sage, and lamb's ears.

My house is painted pale yellow, and my flower garden is on the south side. Should I use yellow, orange, and red to go with the house?

Although the colors are complementary, the warm colors of both the flowers and the house will make the area seem hotter than you'll probably like. Cool colors, like blues, lavenders, and purples, will be a much better choice.

Can I use perennials for their colored foliage alone in my perennial border, even if they have no, or insignificant, blooms?

Yes, plants with colored foliage can be part of the color design scheme, just like flowering plants.

What are some perennial plants grown mainly for foliage color?

Bugleweed, wormwood, rue, lamb's ears, and variegated cultivars of plantain lily, iris, and lily-turf.

Texture and shape

A balance of textures and shapes in the garden makes it more attractive and interesting. When planning the perennial garden, think about the shape, size, and texture of the individual leaves and flowers as well as the overall appearance of the plant.

What are the different types of texture?

Texture may be coarse, medium, or fine. Texture usually refers to the overall appearance of the plant, taking into consideration

Combined astilbe, baby's-breath, daylilies, and peonies make an interesting study in textural contrasts.

Maggie Oster

the plant's form as well as the denseness of the flowers and foliage. For example, leaves may be long and thin, large and round, or some other combination. The actual texture of the foliage and flowers also contributes to its appearance.

What are some perennials with coarse texture?

Bear's-breech, globe thistle, leopard's-bane, perennial sunflower, plantain lily, plume poppy, rose mallow, and saxifrage.

What are some perennials with medium texture?

Bee balm, blue stars, bugloss, butterfly flower, campion, coneflower, lady's-mantle, loosestrife, lupine, pearly everlasting, peony, phlox, purple loosestrife, Solomon's-seal, spurge, stonecrop, and sundrops.

What are some perennials with fine texture?

Astilbe, baby's-breath, basket-of-gold, bleeding-heart, columbine, cranesbill, golden marguerite, hardy pinks, lily-turf, meadow rue, monkshood, ornamental onion, pincushion flower, rock cress, snake grass, thrift, tickseed, torch lily, windflower, wormwood, and yarrow.

What effect does texture have on how I use different perennials?

Texture affects space just as color does. For example, fine-textured plants have a receding effect and can make a shallow border appear deeper. Coarse-textured plants give a feeling of closeness and could be used at the far end of a long border to bring it in closer.

What are some perennials that create a feeling of mass due to their dense foliage, making them ideal as a backdrop to a border?

Carolina lupine, delphinium, false indigo, goatsbeard, meadow rue, perennial sunflower, and rose mallow.

What are the basic forms of flowering plants?

Ground-hugging, vertical, rounded, and open. A flower garden can be composed all of one form, but the most interesting gardens usually alternate and repeat forms.

What are some perennials with a smoothly rounded form, a bushy habit of growth, and dense foliage from top to bottom?

Baby's-breath, blanket flower, bleeding-heart, cranesbill, daylily, false indigo, gas plant, goatsbeard, mist flower, orange sunflower, painted daisy, peony, plantain lily, Shasta daisy, sneezeweed, stonecrop (Autumn Joy and *Sedum spectabile*), tickseed, wormwood.

lamb's ears

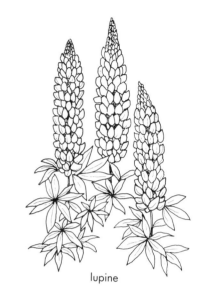

lupine

hosta

columbine

The basic forms of perennial plants are ground-hugging (lamb's ears), vertical (lupine), rounded (hosta), and open (columbine).

Ground-hugging lamb's ears make an excellent border plant in sun or very light shade.

What are some ground-hugging perennial plants that spread across the ground and grow less than eighteen inches tall?

Astilbe, baby's-breath, basket-of-gold, blue plumbago, coralbells, creeping phlox, dwarf bearded iris, hardy pinks, lady's-mantle, lamb's ears, lungwort, plantain lily, primrose, saxifrage, Siberian bugloss, thrift.

What are some perennials that have a vertical accent form?

Astilbe, beard-tongue, bear's-breech, betony, bugbane, Carolina lupine, delphinium, false indigo, foxglove, gay-feather, iris, lobelia, lupine, sage, speedwell, torch lily.

What are some perennials with open, loose form?

Columbine, globe thistle, meadow rue, Oriental poppy, pincushion flower, purple coneflower, rose campion, and snake grass.

Spread (Growth Habit)

More gardeners forget about this aspect of planning and planting a perennial garden than any other, and unfortunately, the mature spread of perennials can be the cause of some of the biggest problems as time goes on. It's hard to imagine that those little pots of flowers may become a four-foot-wide mass in a few short years.

When I got done planting my perennial border last year, it looked so bare that I added extra plants. Now it's a jungle. What do I do?

You'll have to remove some of the plants. Plants spaced too closely not only look jammed in, but they are more prone to diseases due to poor air circulation and must compete for light, water, and nutrients.

You will often have to thin plants fairly brutally as they naturally spread in future years. This often provides opportunities for sharing your garden surplus with friends. In some areas, yearly perennial plant sales afford a chance to exchange favorites, at the same time as to provide a fund-raising event for nonprofit organizations.

After you have considered your site, decided on a color scheme, and determined which plants you'd like to grow, it is time to draw up a garden plan. Although not absolutely necessary, a plan drawn on graph paper will help you to determine more accurately how many plants you need, see potential problems, and maximize the visual impact of the colors, shapes, and textures.

How do I go about creating a scale drawing of a perennial garden?

There is no one "right" way, but the following should get you started. First, make a list, by blooming season, of the perennials you are considering. Mark each one T, M, and S for tall, medium, and short. You might also want to include a code for texture. Some people like to make colored cut-outs of the different plants.

Choose graph paper with either four or eight squares to the inch and allow each square to represent a square foot of garden space. Using a sharp, fine-leaded pencil, first draw the shape of the bed or border you want to plant. Then begin drawing in areas for each of the plants.

How do I know what the garden will look like at different periods during the summer?

To get an idea of how the garden will look at different seasons, use sheets of tracing paper marked for each month or blooming period. Lay them over your main plan. Color in the appropriate areas for that season on each sheet of the tracing paper.

MAKING A GARDEN PLAN

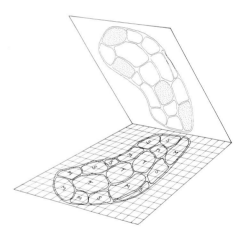

Make a garden plan on graph paper, indicating the heights of plant groupings by marking them T (tall), M (medium), and S (short). Overlay your plan with tracing paper and shade in various areas according to season of bloom and plant color.

2 *Perennials in the Landscape*

reating perennial flower beds for specific purposes or to
meet special needs or restrictions is both a challenge and a
pleasure. The ideas that follow can serve to open limitless
possibilities for the unique gardens you will want to design for
your own home landscape.

What is a flower border?

Borders are at the edge of an area and are approached and
viewed from only one side. Borders might be such plantings as
sweet william along a fence, spurge in front of a hedge, asters
along a driveway, or mixed perennials beside a foundation or
shrub border.

How wide should a border be?

Most borders are three to five feet wide, to make maintenance
as easy as possible. A rule of thumb is to make borders not wider
than one-third their length so that surroundings and length are
in good proportion to one another.

What are perennial beds?

Beds are irregularly shaped "island" gardens, perhaps including a few strategically placed large boulders or a small tree.
Again, this garden is easy to work in, and different effects can be
had from the various sides. In such a garden, it is possible to

DECORATIVE
PLACEMENT OF
PERENNIAL BEDS
AND BORDERS

◀ *A cheerful flower border of daisies, poppies, and dame's-rocket.*

accommodate both sun-loving and shade-loving plants as well as rock garden plants. Or, annuals and perennials can be mixed. If you wish to use only a few plants, apply an attractive mulch or perennial ground cover to fill the remaining spaces.

How large should a bed be?

This depends on the size of the surroundings, for as with borders, the bed should be in scale with the rest of the landscape. Usually any bed that takes up more than one-third of the area in which it is placed looks out of proportion.

Where can I locate perennial beds and borders?

Anywhere you'd like: along terraces, patios, decks, or driveways; in front of fences, walls, or shrubs; next to the foundation; along the walk to the front door. When planning a flower garden, always take into consideration the point from where it will be viewed.

What is the difference between a formal and a naturalistic garden?

Formal design uses straight lines and circular curves or arcs; informal design uses ovals, kidney shapes, or long, free-flowing curves. Formality emphasizes lines; informality emphasizes space, a concept necessary today in low-maintenance gardening. A formal garden need not, however, be large, elaborate, or filled with architectural embellishment.

Which is better suited to a small place, a formal or an informal garden?

Topography controls the type of design to a large extent. Where the ground near the house is flat, a rectangular (formal) type of design is easier to adapt. On rough land, particularly on slopes and in wooded areas, informality is desirable.

Can I use just one perennial as an accent?

The single-accent perennial is very effective, but it must be chosen with great care as it has to be decorative out of bloom as well as in bloom. A dramatic accent that works particularly well is a clump of peonies or daylilies by a garden gate, a grouping of Japanese iris by a small pool, or an ornamental grass against a fence.

Can I use perennials as ground covers?

Very definitely. Perennials should not be overlooked as ground covers for relief from high-maintenance grass. Such perennials as ajuga, lily-of-the-valley, sweet woodruff, and *Sedums* are all visually appealing and quite suitable in the right spot.

Is there really such a thing as a low-maintenance perennial garden?

The answer is a guarded "yes." The best way to achieve such a garden is to select only perennials that require the least amount of maintenance, although some care is always necessary. Particularly appropriate plants are those with the following characteristics:

- division needed no more frequently than every four years (see pages 37-38);
- hardy to -20° F. without winter protection;
- high degree of tolerance to pests, so that spraying is usually not necessary;
- stakes not necessary;
- wide range of soils tolerated;
- leaves either attractive throughout the growing season or die down quickly enough to be hidden by surrounding plants;
- no tendency either to self-sow or to spread by runners so vigorously as to become a nuisance.

What are some of the best perennials for a low-maintenance situation?

Astilbe, balloon flower, betony, blackberry lily, bleeding-heart, blue stars, bugbane, bugloss, butterfly flower, campion, candytuft, Carolina lupine, catmint, coneflower, coralbells, daylily, false indigo, gas plant, globe thistle, goatsbeard, gold-enrod, hardy hibiscus, Jacob's-ladder, knapweed, lady's-mantle, lily-of-the-valley, loosestrife, lungwort, meadow rue, mugwort, Oriental poppy, ornamental grasses, Ozark sundrop, painted daisy, peach bells, peony, pincushion flower, plantain lily, purple loosestrife, sea holly, sea lavender, showy stonecrop, Siberian iris, snake grass, speedwell, Solomon's-seal, sunflower, tickseed, turtlehead, Virginia bluebells, yucca.

What perennials should I be cautious about introducing into my garden because of their tendency to take over?

Some varieties of yarrow (white, in particular), *Campanula persicifolia*, coreopsis, most *Sedums*.

Old-fashioned cutting gardens had the plants set in rows and were not very attractive. Do they have to be made that way?

No. By growing enough plants (a minimum of three) of each perennial in your garden, you should have plenty of flowers to cut for bouquets without destroying the effect of your garden.

What special care does a cutting garden need?

Since you want maximum flower production, regular feeding, watering, and deadheading (see pages 36-37) are especially important.

A LOW-MAINTENANCE PERENNIAL GARDEN

Maggie Oster

Easy-to-grow loosestrife, here shown in a purple variety, is also available with yellow or white flowers.

A PERENNIAL GARDEN FOR CUT FLOWERS

What is the best time and method to gather flowers?

Cut flowers early in the morning, using a sharp knife or scissors and making the stem as long as possible. Choose unblemished flowers that are in various stages of development. Immediately after cutting, plunge the flower stems into a container of tepid water. Put the flowers and container in a cool place for several hours before making your arrangements. Herbs and shrub foliage make fine filler material mixed in with your flowers.

What perennials are particularly nice for bouquets?

Aster, baby's-breath, beard-tongue, bellflower, blanket flower, chrysanthemum, coneflower, coreopsis, delphinium, false dragonhead, gay-feather, globeflower, globe thistle, iris, knapweed, leopard's-bane, lupine, meadow rue, mist flower, monkshood, mugwort, peony, sage, showy stonecrop, sneezeweed, speedwell, sunflower, torch lily, windflower, yarrow.

What are some perennials that produce flowers or seed pods especially adaptable to being dried for bouquets?

Baby's-breath, blackberry lily, Chinese-lantern plant, coralbells, delphinium, false indigo, globe thistle, pearly everlasting, sea holly, sea lavender, yarrow.

PERENNIALS FOR A ROCK GARDEN

I have a sloping area on my property, with a few rock outcroppings. Would such an area be suitable for a rock garden?

Yes, particularly if it is in sun and has well-drained, moderately fertile soil. Even those who enjoy rock gardens, but do not have a slope like yours, can create one by trucking in a few loads of topsoil and rocks.

What kinds of perennials can be planted in a rock garden?

Purists use only those plants found growing naturally on rocky slopes in poor soil, but there are many other low-growing perennials, as well as bulbs, annuals, and shrubs, suited for such a garden. Some of the readily available, easily grown perennials suited for a rock garden situation include basket-of-gold, betony, bishop's hat, blanket flower (Goblin), bugloss, bugleweed, campion, candytuft, Carpathian harebell, coralbells, cranesbill, creeping phlox, cupid's-dart, dwarf baby's-breath, dwarf columbine, dwarf iris, fernleaf bleeding-heart, flax, forget-me-not, hardy pinks, harebell, hen-and-chickens, Jacob's-ladder, lady's-mantle, meadowsweet (Flore Pleno), ornamental grass (blue fescue), plumbago, primrose, purple rockcress, rock cress, saxifrage, sea lavender, Silver Mound, snow-in-summer, speedwell, spurge, stonecrop, sunrose, violet, Virginia bluebells, wild ginger, woolly yarrow.

Are hummingbirds and butterflies attracted by color or scent?

Red, pink, and orange flowers will draw hummingbirds to the garden. Butterflies are attracted by the nectar, often recognized by its scent.

Will caterpillars destroy my garden?

Not necessarily, but if you want butterflies in your garden, you will also have to accept that there will be some foliage damage from their caterpillar stage. You should, of course, use only a minimum of pesticides in the garden if you wish to encourage insects.

What flowers attract hummingbirds?

Bee balm, beard-tongue, bellflower, betony, butterfly flower, campion, catmint, columbine, coralbells, daylily, delphinium, foxglove, globe thistle, hardy pinks, hollyhock, iris, loosestrife, lupine, Oriental poppy, phlox, sage, torch lily.

Maggie Oster

PERENNIALS TO ATTRACT BIRDS AND BUTTERFLIES

Many flowers, including this hardy aster, are especially beloved by hummingbirds and butterflies.

What are some perennials that will attract butterflies?

Bee balm, butterfly flower, coneflower, foxglove, gay-feather, globe thistle, hardy aster, hardy pinks, knapweed, lupine, mist flower, sunflower, sweet rocket.

PERENNIALS FOR A FRAGRANT GARDEN

I want to include as many fragrant-flowered plants as possible in my perennial border. What are some suggestions?

Bee balm, daylily (especially Bonanza, Catherine Woodberry, Earliana, Elizabeth, Holy Grail, Hyperion, Ice Carnival, Lexington, Little Wart, Rozavel, Seneca Moonlet), dropwort, evening primrose, forget-me-not, hardy pinks, lily-of-the-valley, peony (especially White Sands, Dutchess de Nemours, Festiva Maxima, Gardenia, Mary E. Nichols, Alexander Fleming, Edulis Superba, Sarah Bernhardt, Big Ben, Harry L. Richardson), phlox, plantain lily, primrose, sweet pea, sweet rocket, violet.

PERENNIALS FOR A CONTAINER GARDEN

Can perennials be grown in containers?

Yes. They can be grown in anything from ten-inch pots to large planters made of such materials as wood, concrete, clay, or fiberglass. Be sure that there are drainage holes in the bottom of the container, then add a layer of gravel and fill with a soilless potting mix. Feed during the summer with a liquid fertilizer and water frequently, especially in hot dry weather.

Will perennials overwinter in containers?

Possibly, especially in warm climates or regions with a great deal of snow cover. Elsewhere, the roots are likely to be damaged by frozen soil. If there is any doubt about their chances for survival, move container plantings into a cool greenhouse, garage, or cold frame, or group all of them together and cover them with foam insulating blankets and pine boughs.

What are some perennials that grow well in containers?

If a certain plant is particularly special to you, by all means try it in a container. Basically, however, consider those plants and varieties that are compact, form a clump, and bloom over a long period. Some possible perennials include balloon flower, beard-tongue, bellflower, betony, blanket flower, campion, catmint, cinquefoil, coneflower, coralbells, cranesbill, daylily, gas plant, hardy pinks, lady's-mantle, lavender cotton, loosestrife, mallow, painted daisy, phlox, sage, Shasta daisy, Solomon's-seal, speedwell, stonecrop, sundrop, torch lily, violet, yarrow.

Protect container-grown perennials over the winter by covering the pots lightly with foam insulating blankets.

What conditions will most ensure a successful flower garden near the seashore?

Choose a location protected from the wind and salt spray. Enrich the soil as much as possible with organic material such as compost, peat moss, or leaf mold. Seaweed can be used if it has been washed by rain for a season. Water plants frequently during the growing season; mulch and fertilize regularly.

What are some perennials that will do well in a seashore garden?

Baby's-breath, bee balm, betony, blanket flower, bugbane, bugleweed, bugloss, butterfly flower, campion, candytuft, coneflower, coralbells, cupid's-dart, daylily, false indigo, fleabane, foxglove, globe thistle, hardy aster, hardy hibiscus, hardy pinks, hollyhock, leopard's-bane, loosestrife, marguerite, mugwort, ornamental grasses, rock cress, sea holly, sea lavender, spurge, stonecrop, thrift, tickseed, torch lily, yarrow, yucca.

PERENNIALS FOR A SEASHORE GARDEN

3 Planting and Caring for Perennials

Adequate soil preparation, the purchase of healthy plants, proper planting procedures, and regular care will go a long way toward ensuring that your perennial garden will be successful. Time and effort spent now will save having to correct mistakes later.

How shall I prepare new ground for perennials?

Every situation is different. For a precise recommendation for your own unique situation, have your soil tested by your County Extension Service (see page 2). Generally speaking, you should mix in a three- to four-inch layer of well-rotted or dehydrated cow manure, leaf mold, peat moss, or compost, along with ten pounds of superphosphate to 100 square feet. Small gardens can be spaded, but you may wish to rent a rotary tiller for larger areas. You can also add a commercial flower garden fertilizer such as 5-10-10 at the rate recommended on the package.

Should I check and correct the pH of the soil?

A soil test conducted by an outside agency usually includes a pH test, but you can also check it yourself with a kit from the garden center. Most perennials grow best in a slightly acidic soil with a pH of 6 to 7. To raise the pH one point, you need to add ten pounds of lime per 100 square feet of soil. To lower the pH one point, work in three to four pounds of sulfur per 100 square feet.

Healthy plants, such as these white and purple bellflowers tumbling over the bench, and red, pink, and white sweet williams, will result if adequate care is provided.

PREPARING THE SOIL

29

Should I remove all the weeds from the area that is going to be my new perennial bed?

If you are preparing the soil in the fall prior to planting the next spring, the weeds can be tilled in, and they will decompose over the winter. If you are preparing the bed in the spring for immediate planting, remove as many weeds as possible before adding organic matter and spading or tilling.

How deep should the soil be prepared for a new perennial garden?

For best results, the soil should be dug and prepared not less than twelve inches, but eighteen inches will give superior results.

In preparing a perennial garden, should I screen the soil to remove all stones?

No, do not screen the soil, but handpick out any stones larger than a lemon.

Is there any way to change the condition of a poor soil?

Unless the soil condition is extremely unfavorable, almost any soil can be improved with the addition of plenty of organic matter.

Is sand or clay better subsoil for a perennial garden?

Generally speaking, a sandy subsoil is preferable, but if the sand is too loose and porous, drainage will be excessive. If the subsoil is hard-packed clay, drainage will be stopped.

Our soil is sandy. How can we grow perennials?

Add plenty of organic matter, such as manure, compost, or peat moss. Keep the soil fertilized and water heavily when

*A technique known as **double digging** entails removing a spade's depth and width of soil along one row, turning over a spade's depth of soil beneath the top layer, and then digging up the next spade's depth and width of soil and placing it into the first trench. Continue down the length of the bed in this manner and fill in the final row with soil removed from the first row.*

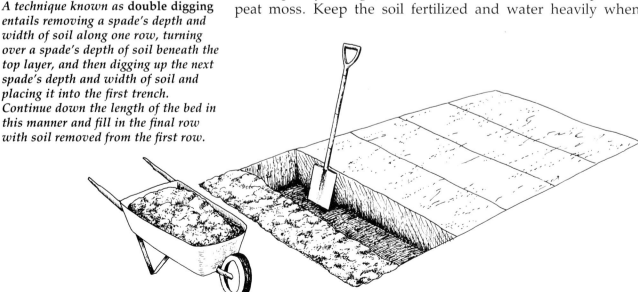

necessary. Plenty of organic matter will be needed for perennials to do best. Choose those perennials that do best in dry, sandy soil.

What makes clay soil so sticky?

Clay is composed of very minute particles, almost the whole surface of which absorbs water. It is this high water content that causes the stickiness. Never work clay when it is wet. It puddles and then hardens, making a poor environment for plant roots. If you dig too soon in the spring you may make your soil practically useless for the entire season.

The soil in my garden is mostly clay. Is there any way I can improve it so that I can grow perennials?

Spade in a three-inch layer of organic material, such as peat moss, compost, or manure, to a depth of six inches.

What is the best method of planting bare-root and container-grown perennials?

With a spade or trowel, make a hole of sufficient size to accommodate the roots without crowding. Remove the container-grown plant from its pot, and put the plant in the hole, placing it no deeper than it grew in the nursery. With your hands, push the soil back in the hole, working it between and over the roots and packing it firmly in. Soak with water.

Should I plant perennials when the soil is sopping wet?

No. Soil structure can be harmed as a result. Wait until the soil is crumbly but still moist.

Should perennials be planted in straight rows or staggered?

The effect is better in a staggered planting. It is also good practice to plant in groups of three.

When is the correct time to plant perennials in the spring? Will they bloom the same year?

Plant as early as the soil can be worked, as soon as possible after receiving them from the nursery. Plants, if large enough, will flower the same season.

I am new to gardening. Should I buy perennials from my local garden center or from mail-order catalogs?

As a new gardener, you may find it easier to select perennials in containers from a garden center. There are at least two advantages: The plants are usually in full growth, so that you can readily see what they look like, and you can set plants out

PLANTING BARE-ROOT AND CONTAINER-GROWN PERENNIALS

To set a container-grown perennial in place, make a hole large enough to accommodate the roots without crowding and deep enough so that the plant sits at the same height it grew in the pot.

any time during the growing season with the least disturbance of their root systems. However, mail-order nurseries are often less expensive and they are likely to offer more kinds of perennials and their varieties than a garden center can.

Container-grown perennials are available at my local garden center from spring until fall, and I am assured that they can be planted anytime during the growing season. Is this true?

Yes. More and more plants (including trees, shrubs, and roses) are being handled in this way. Because the roots of pot-grown plants suffer little disturbance when being transplanted, it is less critical to follow traditional rules to plant them only in the spring and fall.

Should I label my plants after they're planted?

Yes. Note the name of the plant and the planting date on an unobtrusive wood, plastic, or aluminum label to help you keep track of your gardening successes and failures. Such a marker can also keep you from digging into a dormant plant.

Label each new planting with the name of the plant and the date that it was planted.

CARING FOR THE PERENNIAL GARDEN

Can you give me an idea of how much time I'll need to spend taking care of a modestly sized perennial garden?

In general, a perennial garden needs at least some weekly care and maintenance during the summer, with extra hours necessary in spring and fall. Some plants, however, do require less water, fertilizer, pruning, dividing, and pest control than others. Fortunately, the beauty of the garden should make the time you spend caring for it pleasurable, and not particularly strenuous for the most part.

What constitutes good year-round care of a perennial border?

In the spring, when the frost has left the ground, remove the winter mulch. If rotted manure or partly rotted leaves were used, lightly fork the finer portions into the soil, along with a topdressing of complete fertilizer. Reset any plants that were heaved out of the ground by frost. More mulch can be applied to suppress weeds and keep the soil moist and cool, and to keep a crust from forming. Provide support for those plants that need it. Water thoroughly when necessary. Put on more mulch after the first severe frost.

Why do some hardy perennials die off after one or two luxuriant seasons?

There are several possible reasons: most perennials need to be divided and transplanted after two or three years; many are short lived; some do not do very well during the winter; still others succumb to diseases or insects.

Watering

How often should a perennial garden be watered?

Most perennials growing in an "average," humus-rich garden loam need the equivalent of one inch of water each week. A garden in a windy location or one with very sandy soil will need extra water. No definite intervals for watering can be set; the kind of soil and the needs of the various plants, among other factors, have an influence. The soil should be kept moist at all times during the growing season.

How can I determine whether my soil is receiving one inch of water each week?

Use a rain gauge to track rainfall. To check the amount that you are watering, place an empty coffee can halfway between the sprinkler and the furthest point it reaches. Time how long it takes for one inch of water to accumulate in the can. Presuming the water pressure remains constant, run your sprinklers for the amount of time it took for one inch of water to collect in the can.

Why do I need to water my perennials only once a week? Couldn't I sprinkle them lightly every day?

This is the worst thing you could do. Light, frequent watering encourages shallow roots. When it becomes hot or if you go away for a few days, the plants will not be able to survive as well. Deep watering encourages the roots to grow down rather than along the soil surface.

Do you have to water perennial flowers in the winter?

No watering is needed since there is no growth.

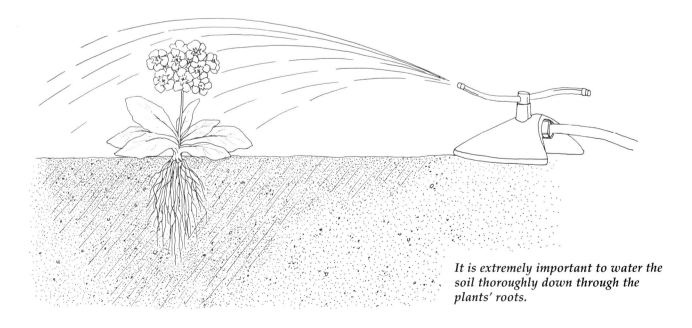

It is extremely important to water the soil thoroughly down through the plants' roots.

Is it true that water should not touch the leaves of perennials?

There is scant danger of water on the leaves doing any harm. Some gardeners believe that there is less risk of fungus growth if, when watering with an overhead sprinkler, you water in early morning so the leaves can dry quickly. On the other hand, if you water in the evening, the moisture has a chance to soak in and last longer without the drying effect of the sun.

Fertilizing

What is a basic fertilizing program for a perennial garden?

Perennials planted in a well-prepared soil should need only spring applications of an organic mulch and 10-10-10 fertilizer. If the fertilizer is dry, sprinkle it on the soil when the soil is moist and the plant's foliage is dry, and then water it into the soil immediately.

What do the numbers on a fertilizer label mean?

The combination 5-10-5, for example, means that the bag contains five-percent nitrogen, ten-percent phosphorus, and five-percent potash; the remainder is inert filler. These elements do not occur in pure form but as compounds with other materials.

Is there anything to be gained by fertilizing perennials during the growing season?

Some plants, such as phlox, delphinium, and chrysanthemums, are helped by supplementary feedings of liquid fertilizers applied when flowers are about to form. Whether or not this is necessary depends on the character of the soil, the initial preparation of the border, and annual routine practices to maintain its fertility.

Are organic fertilizers any better than inorganic ones?

Organic fertilizers can be highly complex, with the nutrients unavailable to plants until they have been digested or broken down into simpler forms by soil organisms. These organisms are partially dormant at temperatures below 60° F. and grow progressively more active up to about 90° F. Thus, organic fertilizers are not too effective in early spring. They have one quality that pure chemical or mineral fertilizers do not: They add organic matter to the soil.

Weeding and mulching

What is the best way to keep down weeds in a perennial border?

Make frequent use of a narrow scuffle hoe to chop off weeds before they attain much size. Run the hoe through the soil about

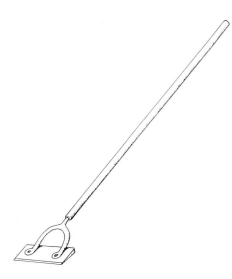

Use a scuffle hoe to chop out weeds before they grow too large.

an inch below the surface. Weeds among the flowers must be pulled out by hand. A mulch of organic materials also helps to keep weeds at a minimum.

How close to my plants should I work the soil, and how deeply can I cultivate it?

The depth depends on the type of plants: shallow-rooted plants need shallow cultivation; deep-rooted plants will take deeper cultivation. You can work close to them all, taking care not to cut their stems.

Will a mulch of organic material, such as straw, grass clippings, compost, cocoa bean hulls, or bark chips, help in weed control?

Yes. Applied in the spring, mulch will keep down weeds, and it will also hold moisture in the soil and help to keep the soil cool.

Are there any tips in applying such a mulch?

Yes, remove any weeds already growing. Spread the mulch two to three inches thick, leaving a small area unmulched around the base of the plant so that the crown is not smothered. Add a sprinkling of 10-10-10 fertilizer to compensate for the extra nitrogen needed for decomposition of the mulch.

Staking

How do I keep certain perennials from falling over, especially when they're in bloom?

Beginning in early spring, stake perennials to keep them from flopping over. A clever English tradition is to put twelve- to eighteen-inch-long (depending on the mature height of the perennial) brushy, woody stems around plants in the spring and allow the perennials to grow up through them. Commercially available, round wire forms on three legs are useful for bushy plants such as Shasta daisy, *Sedums* such as Autumn Joy, or balloon flower, as well as for plants with tall spiky flowers, like delphinium or monkshood. These tall, spiky plants may also be loosely tied to bamboo stakes.

Pinching and disbudding

Why do people pinch back their plants?

Some plants are bushier and sturdier when mature if they are pinched back when they are young. Perennials that benefit from being pinched back are chrysanthemum, hardy aster, sneezeweed, tall-growing speedwell, false dragonhead, and beardtongue, as well as plants like summer phlox that tend to send shoots from the axils of the leaves. Poppies and lilies should not be pinched.

The showy, heavy stems of delphinium may be loosely fastened to bamboo stakes.

Sprawling, weak-stemmed plants such as balloon flower may be staked with brushy stems, put in place when plants are small.

Maggie Oster

Wire forms support these veronicas.

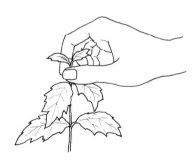

Pinch out the growing tip of such perennials as chrysanthemums and sneezeweed in order to encourage sturdy, bushy growth.

How do I pinch back plants?

Using your thumb and forefinger, remove the top inch or so of growth just above a pair of leaves. This is usually done in April or May. Chrysanthemums need to be pinched several times, but other plants only once.

What is disbudding?

Disbudding involves pinching out some or all of the flower buds when they are about ⅛-inch in diameter, and leaving the main center one so as to have large flowers on a long stem. It is usually done only by people who exhibit such flowers as chrysanthemum.

Deadheading

What does the term deadheading mean?

The technique of removing faded flowers is known as deadheading. Not only does it improve the appearance of many plants, but it also results in repeat bloom for some plants later in the season.

What are some perennials that do not need deadheading?

Bee balm, blackberry lily, blanket flower, butterfly flower, coreopsis, flax, purple loosestrife, the *Sedum* Autumn Joy, snake grass, and sundrops.

What is the best way to divide most perennials?

Dig up the plants and, with the help of two spading forks (or two hand forks if the plant is small), pry the rootstock apart into pieces of suitable size.

When should perennials be divided?

Fall is best, although early spring is a possibility for some plants. Divide early bloomers in early fall, late bloomers in the spring, and bearded iris and Oriental poppies in the summer. Some plants may even be moved about throughout the growing season if you are able to transplant them without greatly disturbing their root systems.

Is August a good month to revamp perennial borders?

Definitely not. It is the hottest and driest month as a rule, and newly transplanted stock (with the exceptions noted below) is likely to suffer.

Which perennials should be moved in midsummer or early fall?

Move bearded iris after it flowers; Oriental poppies in late summer; and bleeding-heart, Christmas rose, and peonies in late summer and early fall.

In northern Maine should perennials be divided and transplanted in fall or spring?

Either one is acceptable, though fall is best, at least four weeks before heavy freezing. In the spring it must be done as early as possible.

Should tall perennials be cut back when they are replanted or transplanted in the fall?

Tall perennials are better if cut back before being moved. Whatever foliage remains down near the soil matters little in the fall.

How do you suggest I rejuvenate my perennial garden?

First, dig up all your perennials in early fall. Obtain a supply of nursery flats or grocery cartons and fill them with the lifted perennials, taking care not to mix up varieties of the same plant. Then spread as much organic material, up to two to four inches

DIVIDING AND TRANSPLANTING PERENNIALS

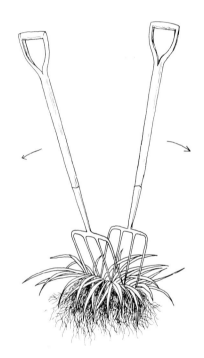

After digging up the plant, divide it by prying it apart with two spading forks.

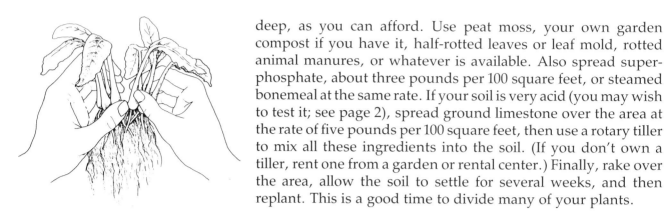

Some plants, such as primrose, need only to be gently pulled apart after being dug up.

deep, as you can afford. Use peat moss, your own garden compost if you have it, half-rotted leaves or leaf mold, rotted animal manures, or whatever is available. Also spread super-phosphate, about three pounds per 100 square feet, or steamed bonemeal at the same rate. If your soil is very acid (you may wish to test it; see page 2), spread ground limestone over the area at the rate of five pounds per 100 square feet, then use a rotary tiller to mix all these ingredients into the soil. (If you don't own a tiller, rent one from a garden or rental center.) Finally, rake over the area, allow the soil to settle for several weeks, and then replant. This is a good time to divide many of your plants.

How important is watering after planting or transplanting perennials?

Watering is crucial to success. Soak the soil well after planting. It's a good idea to add a special transplanting fertilizer or a bit of liquid seaweed or fish emulsion to the water. Continue to water every day for a week or two, unless it rains. After this initial period until winter sets in, water only when the soil is dry.

STARTING PERENNIALS FROM SEED

When is the best time to sow perennial seed either in a greenhouse or indoors under fluorescent lights or in a sunny window?

In late February or early March, using a sterile soilless mix specifically designed for starting seeds. Soon after germination, most kinds of seedlings will be large enough to be transplanted into small individual pots filled with soilless mix. From these small pots, the plants can be set outside directly into soil in a nursery bed (a bed set aside for young plants only) in May. Only the usual summer cultivation is required (see pages 32-35), and strong plants should be available for fall planting in the garden.

Which perennials are easiest to grow from seed?

Blanket flower, hardy pinks, columbine, coneflower, cor-albells, coreopsis, delphinium, flax, fleabane, foxglove, lupine, orange sunflower, primrose, and some bellflowers.

Can perennials be raised successfully from fall-sown seed?

If your winters are severe and you have a cold frame, sow perennial seeds in the fall to give them an earlier start in spring. Be sure to plant them late enough in the season so that they do not germinate. If you try to carry small seedlings through the winter outdoors, losses will be great.

What is the advantage of sowing seed in August?

Some growers sow seed from their own or a neighbor's garden in August in order to secure the advantage of having fresh seed of the current season. However, spring sowing ensures huskier young plants that are better able to face their first winter.

Is it possible to sow seeds of perennials in the open ground?

Yes. Make a special seedbed by mixing fine leaf mold or peat moss and sand into the top three or four inches of soil. Sow as early in May as possible and keep the soil moist. Another good method is to sow into seed pans or flats that are buried to the rims in sand; cover with polyethylene until germination. With either method, transplant when the first true leaves develop. Provide light shade for a few days and water well.

Can any perennials be grown from seed simply by scattering the seeds where they are to bloom?

Success is hit-or-miss. The seeds of certain kinds of perennials, such as foxglove, coreopsis, and garlic chives, that naturally self-sow can be sown this way. These same types can even become a nuisance because of their prolificacy—one of the reasons to deadhead (see page 37).

Easy to grow from seed, masses of brilliant primroses provide welcome early spring color.

Maggie Oster

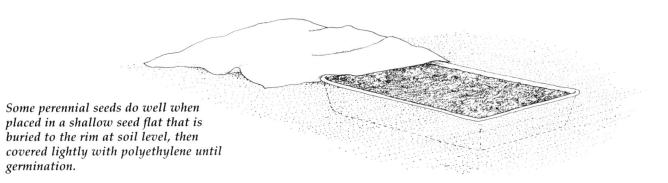

Some perennial seeds do well when placed in a shallow seed flat that is buried to the rim at soil level, then covered lightly with polyethylene until germination.

Can I count on seeds gathered from my own or a neighbor's perennials to produce plants that look like the parent?

It depends on the plant. Seedlings of hybrids and cultivars usually do not look like the parent and are inferior to it. To get an exact duplicate of the parent, these plants are usually propagated by division.

Why do the seeds I save come up so well, while the seeds (especially perennial seeds) I buy do so poorly?

Home-grown seed is usually fresher, and with some perennials this is crucial.

WINTER PREPARATION AND PROTECTION

I have heard that perennials should be cut back in the fall. When, and how much?

In late autumn, when the herbaceous stems have died down, cut the stems of most plants down to within an inch of the soil. Plants with a clump or rosette of green leaves should not be cut off; just cut the old flower stems. Some gardeners prefer to wait until spring before cutting off the tops of the perennials. Their argument is that there is less winter injury from snow and ice with the stems providing some natural protection.

Why are plants covered for the winter?

The rationale for covering plants with some kind of mulch is dependent upon the kind of plant and the climate. Nonhardy plants are covered *before* hard freezing to protect them from low temperatures, because once the plant cells are destroyed, these plants will die. Truly hardy plants are covered after the ground freezes, not to *protect* them from cold, but to *keep* them cold. Where fluctuation of ground temperature results in alternate freezing and thawing, hardy plants are susceptible to injury. Most winterkill occurs in late winter or early spring, for instance, when a mild spell in late winter is followed by a sudden hard freeze. In some cases, shading plants from the winter sun is sufficient. By waiting until after the ground is frozen before you mulch, you allow your plants a chance to harden somewhat, and, hopefully, by very late fall small rodents will have found winter quarters elsewhere.

Shall we let Mother Nature blanket our perennial garden with maple and locust leaves and, if so, when shall we remove the leaves?

Leaves are often used for winter protection, but because they tend to make a sodden mass, they may smother to death any but the most robust plants. Better protection is a loose, light material that does not compact, such as marsh hay, through which air can circulate. Remove the covering gradually when signs of growth are observed underneath. Choose a cloudy day to take off the final covering.

Which perennials need a winter mulch and which prefer none?

Most perennials—except those with heavy green tops, like torch lily—should be mulched, particularly in regions of alternate freezing and thawing. Leaf mold, marsh hay, pine needles, and evergreen boughs are some of the better materials. A covering of about three inches is sufficient for most perennials.

Is it necessary to protect newly planted perennials for the winter? What is the best method?

It is advisable in colder regions to protect all plants over their first winter. Use marsh hay, straw, or evergreen branches, laid on loosely, so as not to smother plants. Do not mulch until after the first hard freeze.

Perennial seeds that I planted in my cold frame in July have made good growth. Can I leave them in the frame until the spring, and if so, should I add a mulch after December?

A mulch will help, but you may want to cover them earlier than December, depending on when you get heavy freezing. Hardy perennials grown from seed sown in July ought to make strong enough plants by late fall not to require cold-frame protection, particularly if planted out in a bed.

4 Prevention and Control of Diseases and Pests

As a group, perennials are neither more nor less affected by diseases and pests than any other plants in the gardens. Although some perennials may be susceptible to a very specific disease or insect, generally those troubles that beset vegetables, herbs, trees, or shrubs are the same ones that affect perennials. It follows then, that control measures are similar. Keep in mind as you read this section that many of the questions and answers will never pertain to your garden, and certainly few of them will ever be a problem at any one time.

Are there ways to minimize disease and pests among perennials?

Yes. First, select those perennials and varieties that are most resistant to diseases and pests that are prevalent in your locality. Second, provide the best possible growing conditions for your perennials, including adequate water, fertilizer, and air circulation, plus proper soil drainage. Third, grow a variety of plants rather than just one type. A garden with variety is less likely to become severely infested, for what troubles one plant does not bother another. Fourth, immediately remove disease- or insect-infested plants or plant parts and destroy them; fall clean-up removes pests that may overwinter and multiply the following season. Finally, treat any problems as soon as they appear, rather than waiting until they become severe.

◀ *Pest- and disease-free gardens result when resistant varieties are planted, optimal growing conditions are provided, and problems are treated as soon as they appear.*

APPLYING PESTICIDES

Please remember these two important rules regarding the use of any pesticides you may be required to use: Always read the fine print on labels to determine what pesticide you are buying, and use them according to the manufacturer's directions.

What are the main spray materials to have on hand? I understand that identical sprays may be available under different names.

This is correct. Pesticides are sold under hundreds of different trade names, but basically the main controls for insects are malathion, carbaryl, *Bacillus thuringiensis*, pyrethrum, rotenone, and insecticidal soaps; and for fungi, they are sulfur, benomyl, and fenaminosulf. Copper sulfate is used mainly for fungi control, but it also kills flea beetles and leafhoppers. Karathane is the main miticide (formulation to kill mites), but insecticidal soaps will also work.

What is a garden duster?

A tool for applying insecticides or fungicides in dry dust form. For the small garden, choose a hand rotary duster or a dust gun, both of which range in size from one-pint to two-quart capacities. Choose one with an extension rod and a flange, which will allow you to stand up while using the duster and yet drive the dust from the bottom of the plant up through it so that the undersides of the leaves are coated. For the larger garden, a knapsack bellows or a rotary duster will save much energy in operation.

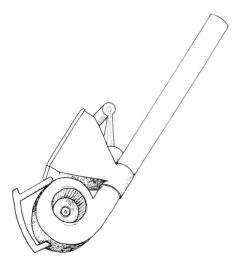

A hand rotary duster with an extension rod permits the operator to drive dust up under the plant.

For pesticides that come in powder form, how do you know how much to use? I tried a dust gun, but the leaves didn't seem sufficiently covered and it was a lot of work. Yet when I tossed the dust by hand it seemed too much.

You need to apply only a thin, even coating of dust, and this can be done only with some sort of duster, never by throwing it on. If yours is too hard to work, either it is of inadequate size and quality for the number of plants you need to treat, or else it needs adjusting. Coverage of the underside of the leaves is most important and can be done only with the right apparatus.

Do you dust plants when they are wet with dew or when they are dry?

There is disagreement over the answer to this question. If ornamental plants are dusted when they are wet, however, a conspicuous and unattractive residue remains.

What are garden sprayers?

Equipment to apply liquid pesticides in a fine mist. Sprayers vary from pint- or quart-size atomizers to huge power apparatus. For the average garden, a back-carried, cylindrical, com-

A back-carried, cylindrical, compressed-air sprayer.

pressed-air sprayer or a knapsack sprayer of one and one-half- to three-gallon capacity will be sufficient.

No sprayer is better than the care given it. Immediately after each use, rinse the sprayer thoroughly, and occasionally take it apart for cleaning. Extra parts can often be obtained from manufacturers or distributors to keep old sprayers in operation. It is a good policy to keep and label separate sprayers for each different product you use so as not to mix dangerous chemicals.

Is a hose proportioner type of sprayer sufficient for a home gardener?

Hose sprayers of the proportioner type are very convenient and easy to use. Solutions and emulsions are readily handled, but the undissolved particles in suspensions may cause clogging. Further, not all types give a suitable dispersion of the active chemical in the spray. Those with a shut-off near the nozzle are much preferable to those that have no shut-off, requiring you to place your finger over a hole to start the chemical mixing with the water spray.

Hose proportioners add specified amounts of chemical pesticide to water as it flows from the hose.

What is an insecticide?

Chemical compounds that are used in the control of insects are generally called insecticides, which are grouped according to their main modes of action: a *stomach poison* attacks the internal organs after being swallowed; a *systemic insecticide* is a stomach poison that has been absorbed into the sap of plants; a *contact insecticide* kills upon contact with some external portion of the insect's body; a *residual-contact insecticide* kills insects by foot contact for long periods after application; a *fumigant* is a chemical that produces a killing vapor in the air; and a *repellent* is a substance that is distasteful or malodorous enough to keep insects away.

Of the various insecticides available, pyrethrum and insecticidal soaps are contact poisons. Rotenone kills both as a stomach and as a contact poison. Malathion and carbaryl, known commercially as Sevin, readily destroy many chewing and sucking insects.

How are insects affected by insecticides?

Contact poisons usually work through their action on the spiracles (breathing apparatus) of insects. Chewing insects have jaws and bite holes in plant tissue; hence, they can be controlled by stomach poisons. Sucking insects obtain their food through a beak that pierces the plant to get at its sap, so therefore these insects can be killed only by systemic or contact poisons.

What are insecticidal soaps?

For many years, regular household soap was used as an insecticide. In recent years, this concept has been taken to a

INSECTS AND THEIR CONTROL

·

more refined level with the creation of specially prepared, pure soaps from natural fatty substances. These commercially available insecticidal soaps kill many insects on contact without damaging plants or harming people, animals, or beneficial insects such as honeybees and lady beetles; they are completely biodegradable and have no toxic aroma. Some insects that can be controlled with insecticidal soaps include aphids, mealybugs, whitefly, mites, earwigs, slugs, and scale.

What are biological insecticides?

They are naturally occurring insect diseases that can be produced commercially and formulated for application as sprays or dusts in the same manner that chemical insecticides are handled. They include two spore-forming bacteria, *Bacillus popillia* (milky spore disease) for Japanese beetle, and *Bacillus thuringiensis* (Dipel, Thuricide, Baktur), which is effective against various caterpillars, such as cabbage looper, gypsy moth, and bagworm. Their toxic specificity makes them safe to use around food, water, and animals. When the susceptible insects feed on the treated plant, the pests consume spores that inflict them with fatal disease.

I often see the name dicofol suggested for mites. What is it?

Dicofol is the accepted common name for Kelthane, a very effective and widely available miticide for spider mites on ornamental plants.

I have a cat and dog that roam around in my gardens. Will malathion sprays applied to the plants harm them?

Very unlikely. Malathion is one of the least toxic insecticides to warm-blooded animals. In addition, it loses its toxic properties rapidly upon exposure to air, so that in two days no toxic residue is left. Do keep pets and children away from freshly sprayed plants. Honeybees may be killed with malathion.

What is pyrethrum?

A contact insecticide obtained from the pyrethrum plant, which is a chrysanthemum, mostly grown in Africa. It is especially effective against aphids and soft-bodied insects, but it will kill whatever chewing insects it hits, including beetles, leafhoppers, whiteflies, caterpillars, and stinkbugs. It is useful for spraying flowers, because it leaves no stain.

What is rotenone?

The principal insecticidal constituent in the roots of such plants as *Derris* or *Lonchocarpus*. It acts as both a stomach and a contact poison for insects, and kills fish and other cold-blooded animals. It may be considered far less injurious to people than other pesticides, although it is often a throat irritant. It leaves no poisonous residue on the plant. Rotenone formerly was obtained from the Far East, but it is now produced in South America. Rotenone dust is available in a one-percent dilution.

Is Sevin safe to use?

Carbaryl, sold under the brand name of Sevin, is a very useful, broad-spectrum insecticide that is comparatively safe for both plants and the user. It suppresses or controls some rust and gall mites. It does kill bees and some other beneficial insects and can increase the spider mite problem, because it kills the mites' natural predators. Look for sprays that include a miticide.

What insects are harmless in the garden?

Of the harmless, or even helpful ones, lady beetles, ground beetles, and praying mantises are most often seen in the home garden. A sluglike creature, larva of the syrphid fly, also occasionally feasts upon aphids.

Lady beetle.

I have found several black, brown, and iridescent large beetles in the ground this fall. Are they harmful?

No, you probably found ground beetles, which have very prominent jaws and live in the earth or under stones. These are beneficial insects, feeding on cankerworms and other pests, and should not be disturbed.

I have often heard that praying mantises are helpful to have in the garden. Can you tell me something about them?

If praying mantises are not naturally present in your neighborhood—these ferocious-looking, but beneficial insects are not commonly found much north of 40° latitude—you may not be able to introduce them successfully. A member of the grasshopper family, the praying mantis is very long and thin, with prominent eyes and enormous front legs, often held up in a praying attitude and used for catching other insects, such as aphids, mites, and caterpillars.

Praying mantis.

Are ants harmful in the garden?

Ants are undesirable not because they afflict the plants themselves, but because they loosen the soil around the roots when they feed and thus cause the plants to wilt and die. In addition, they carry and nurse aphids and mealybugs for their honeydew. Apply either Sevin (carbaryl) or malathion to their nests to kill them.

What control program would you suggest for aphids?

Aphids are soft-bodied, sucking insects that often cluster at the tips of new growth, causing the leaves to curl. Their active

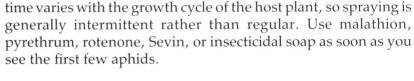

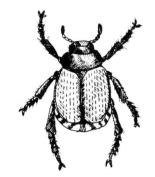

Aphids are extremely common sucking insects that often cluster at the tips of new growth.

Japanese beetle.

Twelve-spotted beetle.

time varies with the growth cycle of the host plant, so spraying is generally intermittent rather than regular. Use malathion, pyrethrum, rotenone, Sevin, or insecticidal soap as soon as you see the first few aphids.

Can anything be done to destroy the white aphids that feed on the roots of plants?

Pour a solution of malathion (one tablespoon to a gallon of water) into a depression around the plant's stem. Root aphids are usually tended by ants, so that ant control should also be started (see above).

What are the hard-shelled insects that are devouring my perennials?

These are probably some type of beetle, a large group of insects with chewing mouth parts and hardened front wings that form convex shields. Except for a few beneficial types, such as ground and lady beetles, they are injurious both in their grub, or larval, stage and as adults. Control them by stomach or contact poisons such as Sevin or rotenone used in the ground or on the foliage.

What are effective ways to suppress Japanese beetles?

There are several techniques for fighting this one-half-inch-long, shiny metallic green beetle that is such a severe pest in some areas. First, from the end of June through the end of September, spray with carbaryl, rotenone, or pyrethrum to attack the adult beetles. The frequency and number of applications depends greatly on the amount of new growth, but weekly sprays are sometimes necessary. Another popular method is to handpick beetles and drop them into a jar or can of kerosene. Milky spore disease treatment on the lawn is an effective long-term control measure, but it takes several years for this to have a major effect on the beetle population. Finally, special traps may be placed at strategic locations around the property. As with the milky spore treatment, this technique may take several years before results are noticed.

What can be done about twelve-spotted beetles? They ruin all the late blooms in my garden.

Twelve-spotted cucumber beetles are hard to kill, but dusting or spraying with carbaryl or rotenone is often helpful.

How can I combat flea beetles?

Flea beetles, which get their name from their habit of quickly springing several inches when disturbed, are small, black, oval beetles that chew tiny holes in the foliage of many garden plants. Dust or spray your plants with carbaryl or rotenone for control of these insects.

How can borers be prevented from doing their deadly work?

Borers are caterpillars or grubs, the larvae of moths or beetles, that work in woody or herbaceous stems. They are best prevented by burning old stalks of your plants at the end of the growing season. Destroy as many borers as possible by hand and use malathion at two-week intervals for control during the growing season.

The leaves of my plants have big holes, with a few worms, which I suspect did the damage. Do you agree?

The ''worms,'' more properly called caterpillars, are the larvae of various butterflies, moths, and certain sawflies. Most insecticides will control them, but the safest method is to use *Bacillus thuringiensis*.

Leafhopper.

In July, when I approached some of my perennials, myriads of small insects came flying out. What were they?

They probably were leafhoppers, which can damage your plants. Green to yellow and only about one-eighth inch long, they are active fliers when disturbed. Control them with pyrethrum or malathion.

While digging in the ground recently, I saw quite a few slender, black insects about two inches long that looked like tiny, thousand-legged snakes. What could they be, and are they injurious to plants?

These are probably millipedes—meaning thousand-legged—although literally they have about fifteen pairs of legs. They are usually beneficial in the garden, preying on other insects, but they sometimes enlarge on damage begun by other insects.

Millipede.

Do earthworms (or angle worms) feed on and destroy peony, iris, and other tubers? I have dug them up and found worms embedded in the tubers, with nothing left but the outer shell.

Your peony probably succumbed to botrytis blight, and the iris, to borers and rot. Earthworms do not feed on living plant tissue, but are an important part of healthy, humus-rich soil.

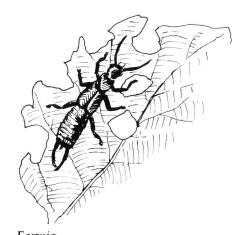

Earwig.

Is there any way to exterminate earwigs?

There is little that can be done to exterminate earwigs, those beetlelike insects that may be scattered all around the yard. Trap them under boards, and then throw them into a can of kerosene, or spray them with insecticidal soap, pyrethrum, or malathion.

What are the fuzzy white bugs on my flowers?

They sound like mealybugs, which are sucking insects closely related to scale. Wash off your plants with a strong spray from the hose. Then, spray with insecticidal soap or malathion.

Mealybug.

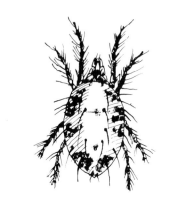

Spider mite.

Cyclamen mite.

What can be done to avoid or control mites?

Three kinds of mites are apt to be troublesome in the garden: spider mites, gall and rust mites, and cyclamen mites. Because they are microscopic in size, a hand magnifier is necessary to identify them as a problem. If you notice webbing on the undersides of leaves or between needles, or stippled or yellowed foliage, mites may be present. Spider mites are actually encouraged by the use of carbaryl (Sevin), because it kills many of the mites' natural predators as well as some of the mites. They can be partially checked by washing the foliage with strong jets of water and spraying with insecticidal soap or dicofol (Kelthane).

What are nematodes?

Nematodes are roundworms or eelworms, too small to see with the naked eye. They live in moist soil, in decaying organic matter, or as parasites in living plant tissues. They can travel only a short distance in the soil by themselves but are spread when surface water moves infested soil from place to place, and, very commonly, by local transfer and shipment of infested plants. Nematodes are particularly prevalent in sandy soils in southern states and in California. In the North, they may live during the winter in perennials and can also survive free in the soil.

How do you recognize the presence of nematodes?

Injury to plants is slow to show up and not at all dramatic. Usually, conspicuous above-ground symptoms do not appear until a heavy population of nematodes has built up. Nematodes should be suspected when plants show a slow decline in vigor and growth, when they become stunted and spare, when water does not help them much in drought, or when the foliage becomes discolored yellow or bronze. The plants' feeder roots may be lacking and the root system stunted and sparse or matted and shallow.

How are nematodes controlled?

Remove seriously infested plants. Cut off all plant tops after bloom. Make cuttings or divisions only from healthy plants, and either plant in a new location or sterilize the soil with a nematocide. The most effective nematocides, however, must be applied only by a certified applicator using specialized equipment. A good preventive against nematodes is to plant marigolds; their scent repels the insects.

Is there any way to rid my garden of slugs?

No, but they can be suppressed or minimized by a combination of good sanitation practices and the proper use of slug baits or traps. During the daytime, slugs and snails hide in the dark in

Slug.

very moist spots beneath stones, boards, and trash on the ground and in the soil. In a well-tilled garden, free of weeds and uncluttered by stones, stakes, and plant refuse, slugs will have few places to thrive.

Two slug baits sold under various trade names are metaldehyde and Mesurol. Mesurol should not be used around food plants (if you interplant flowers and vegetables), but metaldehyde may be. Be sure to follow label directions carefully when treating the soil, and do not treat plants directly.

Traps may be the best approach for small gardens. Place wooden boards in the garden to serve as hiding places. When you overturn them, you will find a multitude of slugs, which can then be eradicated. Alternatively, fill shallow dishes with beer and bury them to the rim at soil level, forming traps that slugs will crawl into and drown. Finally, sprinkle salt or lime directly onto slugs to kill them.

Thrip.

How can thrips be controlled?

Most thrips are small, slender insects, one-sixteenth inch long and only as wide as a small needle. They suck out the sap in leaves, causing a mottled appearance. Pyrethrum, rotenone, and carbaryl can be used as controls.

What is the black beetle that is so destructive to the petals of many of my perennials?

The black blister beetle is a common pest of hardy asters and chrysanthemums, particularly, as well as of other flowers. Unfortunately, it does prefer the petals to the leaves. Kill the beetles with stomach poisons or contact insecticides or by brushing them into cans of kerosene. Avoid touching the insects, as their secretions can cause a blister.

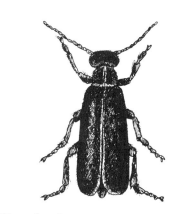

Blister beetle.

Can I recognize fungi on my plants by sight?

Fungi are members of the order of lowest plants, subsisting on both decaying and living tissue. Some fungi are readily recognized at a glance: mildew, with its white weft of threadlike fibers growing over a leaf; rust, which produces reddish dusty spore pustules; and smut, with its masses of black spores. Some can be differentiated only by microscopic examination.

What is a fungicide?

A material used to eradicate fungi in the soil or on seeds or plants. It is also used as a protectant to cover susceptible plant parts before the disease organisms appear. Some fungicides frequently used on perennials include benomyl (Benlate), copper sulfate-hydrated lime (bordeaux mixture), ferbam, folpet, and sulfur.

FUNGI
AND FUNGICIDES

What is benomyl?

Benomyl is sold under the tradename Benlate. As a systemic fungicide, it is taken up into the vascular system of the plant and is excellent for control of powdery mildew and other fungi.

What is bordeaux mixture?

An old-fashioned fungicide still of value in the control of plant diseases. It is a mixture of copper sulfate and hydrated lime. Bordeaux mixture may be purchased in dry powder form to be mixed with water at the time of spraying or it may be made at home by thoroughly dissolving three ounces of copper sulfate (bluestone) in three gallons of water. Add five ounces of hydrated lime, and mix completely.

What amount of powdered bordeaux mixture should be mixed in per gallon of water?

The directions come on the package, but usually eight to twelve tablespoons of prepared, dry bordeaux powder to one gallon of water. For spraying of most ornamental plants, about half this amount is safer, less conspicuous, and equally effective.

Haven't ferbam and folpet been around a long time as fungicides?

Yes, these belong to a group of fungicides, all of which were first developed in the 1930s and 1940s. They control a broad range of fungus diseases and are very popular for home garden use. Ferbam is less toxic than folpet.

Is sulfur a fungicide?

Both elemental sulfur and lime-sulfur are effective in controlling many common fungal pests of plants, including powdery mildew and leaf spot. The lime-sulfur also helps to control spider mites, but it leaves a residue and stains painted objects, such as houses, fences, walls, and trellises. Neither product should be used when the air temperature is above 85° F. Sulfur is available as a dust, a ready-to-use spray, and as a concentrate for dilution as a spray.

What is the white powdery substance on the leaves of plants?

This is powdery mildew. It is most prevalent on phlox, delphinium, and chrysanthemum, but affects other perennials as well. Good air circulation around plants will help. Use benomyl or sulfur for control.

What will prevent crown rot?

Crown rot is a disease causing sudden wilting of plants from a rotting at the crown (the point where the plant stem and roots merge). A fungus called *Sclerotium rolfsii* is the cause, and the

Powdery mildew is common on such plants as delphinium, phlox, and chrysanthemum.

best prevention is to put healthy plants in a new location. The fungus may live for several years in the soil in the form of reddish-tan sclerotia, which resemble mustard seeds. Therefore, when the diseased plant is removed, it is important to take out all surrounding soil to a depth of one foot, and two feet or more wide, and replace it with fresh soil. If crown rot is a major problem, you should have the soil professionally sterilized.

What causes new growth to die back and spots with raised borders to appear on leaves?

You're describing anthracnose, or leaf spot. This is most likely to occur on chrysanthemum, columbine, daylily, hollyhock, delphinium, monkshood, violet, peony, and phlox. Remove and destroy diseased foliage. Chemical sprays are not always effective, but folpet sometimes works.

What is blight?

There are many different kinds of this plant disease, with a variety of appearances, but basically leaves become spotted or disfigured with lesions, a gray mold appears, and buds wither and do not open. Remove and destroy all diseased parts of the plants immediately. Benomyl and ferbam may be used as chemical controls.

The leaves of some of my plants are mottled and their growth is stunted. What might the reason be?

Very possibly some form of mosaic, caused by a virus. Perennials most often affected include chrysanthemum, dianthus, delphinium, iris, and primrose. There is no remedy. Plants should be destroyed. Virus diseases are sometimes spread by aphids, so controlling these will help. Also, select virus-free or virus-resistant varieties.

What is rust on plants?

True rust is a fungus that appears as reddish-brown or reddish-orange pustules of spores, or, in the case of red-cedar and apple rust, in long, gelatinous spore horns. Very often gardeners speak of rust when they merely mean a reddish discoloration of the tissue, which might be due to a variety of causes other than the true rust fungus.

Even after being watered, one of my perennials stayed wilted. Why was this?

The plant was affected by one of the two wilt diseases, fusarium or verticillium, where the water supply is cut off to either the entire plant or a part of it. The only solution is to remove the affected part or the entire plant. Do not try to grow the same kind of plant in the same place for two or three years.

ANIMALS

Do you have any advice on keeping dogs away from my perennial flower beds and borders?

Owners should be willing to keep their dogs restrained and, when walking them on a leash, should keep them curbed rather than allowing them to ruin plantings near a sidewalk. Moth balls and the various chemicals sold as dog repellents in garden centers may help.

What is the best way to control California pocket gophers?

There are many species of the pocket gophers (ground rats) found in California, Oregon, and Washington. There are special gopher traps on the market. Consult your County Extension Agent for regional restrictions and recommendations for available baits.

How do I get rid of moles?

It is unfortunate that moles, which really do a lot of good in the world by eating white grubs and other insects, should also have the bad habit of making unsightly ridges and mounds in gardens and disturbing the roots of flowers and vegetables by their tunnels. Feeding on the plants is actually done by mice that use the mole runs. There are not many nonpoison, nontrap options for control. A cat will discourage both moles and mice. Commercially available traps and poisons are effective control measures. Another method is get rid of the white grubs that attract the moles.

What is a good rabbit repellent?

The New Jersey Fish and Game Commission has listed nine repellents for harassed gardeners: (1) dust plants, when damp, with powdered lime; (2) dust liberally with dusting sulfur; (3) sprinkle plants with red pepper; (4) spray with a solution of three ounces of Epsom salts in one gallon of water; (5) spray with one teaspoon of Lysol in one gallon of water; (6) spray with two teaspoons of Black Leaf 40 in one gallon of soapy water; (7) spray with a solution of common brown laundry soap; (8) spray with one ounce of tartar emetic and three ounces of sugar in one gallon of water; (9) sprinkle naphthalene flakes between the plants. One of the easiest methods is the family's pet cat!

I want to attract birds to my garden, but squirrels always monopolize my feeding stations. Do you have any suggestions?

If the feeding station is hung from a horizontal wire, metal guards can be placed on either side; or if the feeding station is on top of a post, a guard can be placed underneath. If the feeder is anywhere within leaping distance of the ground, shrubbery, or trees, however, a guard is useless. You may simply have to put out enough food for the squirrels as well as for the birds.

How do I get rid of chipmunks?

These ground squirrels, which eat some slugs and insects, should not be destroyed without reason. To protect bulbs against chipmunks, plant your bulbs in wire baskets. Cats will also discourage chipmunks.

Is there any practical way to get rid of mice in the garden?

Not really, and what little can be done is only moderately helpful at best. Snap traps are the best and safest method. Cats that are good mousers help, but winter snows, as well as mulches, provide mice with protection. Consult your local extension agent for recommendations and currently available products.

Where can I turn for further help in diagnosing the pests and diseases that I suspect might be troubling my garden?

Your county Extension Service, often associated with a state land-grant university, is set up to give you exactly that advice. A wealth of valuable information is readily available through a visit or phone call to the local county agent of this educational arm of the U.S. Department of Agriculture. Phone and address listings for Extension Services can usually be found under county name in local phone directories.

How do I know that a pesticide is safe for home use?

Federal, state, and local laws regulate the sale and use of pesticides and at the same time help to protect both the public from dangerous residues and the environment from deleterious hazards. The Environmental Protection Agency approves specific pesticides, as well as their label directions, and any use inconsistent with these directions is then illegal under federal and state laws. Home gardeners often misuse pesticides by applying more, and more often, than the recommended rate, by treating when unnecessary, and by improperly disposing of toxic wastes in such places as sewage systems, storm drains, or sites where runoff ends up in streams or other bodies of water.

FURTHER HELP

5 Favorite Perennials

Adam's needle. See Yucca.

Amsonia. See Blue stars.

Astilbe *(Astilbe)*

Is the astilbe that flowers in the late spring and early summer related to spirea, the shrub?

No, but many nurseries and catalogs cause confusion by persistently labeling these herbaceous perennials—which are decidedly nonwoody—as "spirea." Like some spirea, the pink, rose, red, or white blossoms are fluffy. The common varieties grow eighteen inches to three feet tall and are hardy to -30° F.

I would like to grow astilbe plants in my flower garden, but I've been told that they require constantly wet soil. Is this true?

While the plants of astilbe revel in moist, rich soil, they also adapt to more average conditions. When planting, add good compost, leaf mold, or peat moss to the planting holes so that soil moisture will be retained. Astilbes usually do best in light shade, except in cool climates.

How do I propagate astilbes?

Large clumps may be propagated by division in the spring.

◄ *Bright-colored blanket flowers are easy to grow from seed, tolerate drought, and bloom almost continuously from late spring to fall.*

Ann Reilly

Astilbe: Grow astilbe in light shade unless your summers are rather cool.

Avens *(Geum)*

The avens I planted several years ago produced lovely orange-red flowers the first year or so, then they died out. What happened?

The most common varieties of avens are short lived. Try growing Borsii, Georgenberg, Heldreichii, and Starker's Magnificent.

Under what conditions will avens grow best?

They need rich, well-drained, moist soil, in partial shade. With winter mulch, most are hardy to -10° F. or slightly colder. Propagate by division.

Baby's-breath *(Gypsophila)*

Where should baby's-breath be planted in the garden?

It will grow in any reasonably good soil that is well drained, deeply cultivated, and not more than slightly acid. Plants need full sun and lots of space. Plant tall baby's-breath among spring bulbs or early-blooming perennials so that its lush growth hides the dying foliage of the spring plants.

Can baby's-breath be successfully transplanted?

Yes. Do so in the spring, and take care not to break the fleshy roots.

How is baby's-breath propagated?

Propagation is done by division, by cuttings, or by grafting on pieces of roots.

Does baby's-breath need to be staked?

Those kinds that grow over eighteen inches tall should be staked. Consider using one of the galvanized-wire rings made for this purpose, as they are sturdy and fairly unobtrusive.

Which baby's-breath is best for bouquets?

The double forms are the best for cutting and drying for use during winter months. Any of the varieties are excellent cut flowers. If the flowers are cut back before they go to seed, plants will usually bloom again.

Does baby's-breath have to be mulched in winter?

Baby's-breath is hardy to -40° F., but at these temperatures a loose winter mulch is recommended.

Balloon flower (*Platycodon*)

Does balloon flower need a rich soil?

No, any open, well-drained garden soil will suit it. Plant balloon flower in the spring, with the crown barely covered with soil.

Do balloon flowers need winter protection?

They are hardy to -40° F. and generally need no protection, although mice may eat their roots.

Are balloon flowers difficult to transplant?

Yes. They have long, fleshy roots, so you must take care when digging not to break them. The roots of old plants often go down eighteen inches or more; young plants are easier to move.

How is balloon flower propagated?

By careful division in the spring, or by seed sown in the fall or spring. Fortunately, balloon flower needs infrequent division, for it is not as simple as for most fibrous-rooted perennials. Cut off the outer sections of the thickened crown so that both buds and roots are present on each division. Dust cuts with fungicide to prevent infection.

I have been told that balloon flowers are slow to appear in the spring. Is this so?

Yes, they are one of the last perennials to appear above the ground. It's best, therefore, to mark their location in the fall so as to avoid injuring the plants in the spring before they emerge.

Basket-of-gold, Goldentuft (*Aurinia*)

What is the cascading plant with yellow flowers?

This is basket-of-gold. With its evergreen gray foliage and low growing habit, it is at its best planted in full sun, in very well-drained, neutral to alkaline soil. Use it at the top of a wall, at the front of a flower border, or along rocks. It is hardy to -40° F. After the plants flower, cut them back by a third. Propagate by dividing roots or from cuttings.

Why does basket-of-gold die?

Possibly because of "wet feet." Good soil drainage is necessary; the roots should never stand in water. This plant thrives on stone walls and in other dry locations. Because they are alpines, the plants are not long lived where summers are hot and humid.

Basket-of-gold: This low-growing plant thrives in dry locations.

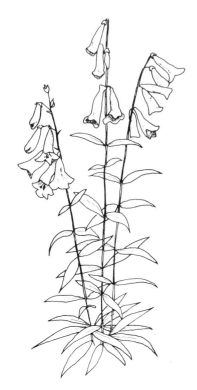

Beard-tongue: Encourage neat growth by staking beard-tongue when it is about a foot tall.

Beard-tongue, Penstemon *(Penstemon)*

Is penstemon a hardy plant?

Hardy to -40° F., beard-tongue grows eighteen to thirty-six inches tall with spikes of scarlet, pink, or purple foxglovelike flowers in summer. Of the more than 250 different species of *Penstemon,* many remain green until long after frost appears. They need a very well-drained soil that is not particularly rich.

How do you trim and care for penstemons?

They need no trimming, but the wiry stems of the tall kinds need support, best supplied by twiggy brush inserted among the plants when they are about a foot tall. Tie loose stems to the brush and cut the tops of the brush away when flower buds form. Cut down the stems after bloom and top-dress with bone meal.

What is the best way to divide penstemon plants?

Remove the plants from the ground in early spring, pull them gently apart, and replant.

Bear's-breech *(Acanthus)*

My bear's-breech seldom bears the spikes of purple flowers it's supposed to. What can I do?

Bear's-breech prefers cool and dry, but sunny conditions. To survive in areas with hot summers, it must be grown in shady spots where it is cool and moist, but these conditions unfortunately keep it from blooming well.

Our winter temperatures go to -20° F. Will bear's-breech grow for me?

Bear's-breech is reliably hardy only to 10° F., but with well-drained soil and a heavy winter mulch, you may be successful.

How do I propagate bear's-breech?

Bear's-breech is easily increased by division of the roots. In fact, in California bear's-breech spreads so rapidly that the roots should be confined. Plants may also be started from seed.

Seemingly overnight there are slimy trails on the leaves of my bear's-breech and big portions have been bitten out of them. What is causing this?

Slugs and snails. Set out shallow pans of beer or use commercial slug bait.

Bee balm, Bergamot *(Monarda)*

I love the unusual flowers of bee balm, as do bees and hummingbirds, but I've had trouble keeping plants. What might be wrong?

Bee balm is easily grown if conditions are right. Hardy to -30° F., plants grow three feet tall in humus-rich, moist soil in full sun or light shade. Plants do not live long in areas with warm winters or dry soil. They should be divided every couple of years. To prevent pests from overwintering in the plants, cut them to the ground in fall and destroy the debris.

Bellflower, Canterbury-bells *(Campanula)*

What growing conditions do bellflowers require?

Provide them with fertile, humus-rich, and moist but well-drained soil. They prefer full sun except in hot climates, where they do better in light shade. A winter mulch may be necessary. In general, the bellflowers are relatively pest-free. Where slugs and snails may be a problem, put out shallow pans of beer or commercial bait. Divide plants every three or four years. Propagate by division or cuttings. Taller varieties may need staking.

I have problems with canterbury-bells rotting away, even in dry soil. What is the problem?

There are two soil fungi that may cause crown or stem rot under moist conditions, but your trouble may actually be due to insufficient water. Try another location in improved soil mixed with organic matter, such as leaf mold, compost, or peat moss.

Maggie Oster

Bellflower: Canterbury-bells **(Campanula Medium)** *are the showiest and best known of all bellflowers.*

SELECTED BELLFLOWERS

Carpathian harebell *(C. carpatica)* grows in twelve-inch mounds of crinkled, pointed, semievergreen leaves and bears blue or white upward-facing, open bell-shaped flowers in midsummer. Remove faded flowers for continuous bloom. Plant in cool, moist, well-drained soil, in the rock garden, in front of the flower border, or along paths.

Canterbury-bells *(C. Medium* and *C. Medium calycanthema),* the showiest and best known of the bellflowers, is a biennial. It bears two-inch white, pink, blue, or purple flowers on stalks two feet tall.

Peach-leaved bellflower *(C. persicifolia)* bears stately two- to three-foot spikes of blue or white,

cup-shaped flowers throughout summer from a mound of long, narrow leaves. It can become very weedy in some areas, but the flowers are excellent for cutting. Carpathian harebell, danesblood, and peach-leaved bellflower are all hardy to -40° F.

Danesblood *(C. glomerata)* has upward-facing clusters of twelve to eighteen bell-shaped flowers on a one- to three-foot stem in midsummer.

Scotch harebell *(C. rotundifolia),* often found wild in parts of Europe, Asia, and North America, is a dainty plant about twelve inches tall with wiry branches of one-inch, deep blue bells during summer. It does best in cool climates.

Bergamot. See Bee balm.

Betony, Lamb's ears *(Stachys)*

Is betony really related to lamb's ears? They look so different.

They are indeed. Betony *(S. grandiflora)* has rippled, dark green leaves with scalloped edges; the rosy-mauve, eighteen-inch flower spikes develop in July. Lamb's ears *(S. byzantina)* is a wonderful edging plant, with soft, furry, silver-gray leaves; growth is ground-hugging, with spikes of small magenta flowers growing eighteen inches tall.

How hardy are lamb's ears and betony?

Lamb's ears is hardy to -30° F. and betony is hardy to -40° F.

What kind of soil and light does *Stachys* need?

Any good, well-drained garden soil and full sun or very light shade.

How is *Stachys* propagated?

By dividing in the fall or spring, or by seed.

Bishop's hat *(Epimedium)*

How is bishop's hat best used?

It makes an excellent ground cover and is fine for rock gardens, with its attractive foliage and tiny, unusual, pink, white, or yellow flowers in early spring. It is especially nice among the small spring-flowering bulbs, such as grape hyacinth, scilla, and aconite. Plant it where it is lightly shaded and has rich, moist soil. Most varieties grow one foot tall and are hardy to -30° F. Propagate by division.

Bishop's weed. See Snow-on-the-mountain.

Blackberry lily *(Belamcanda)*

I have a plant with an unusual seed pod that resembles a blackberry. Can you tell me what it is?

You're describing blackberry lily. Its long-lasting, six-petaled, star-shaped flowers may be orange, yellow, or apricot with darker speckles. The gray-green foliage resembles that of iris. Plants are hardy to -20° F. and grow one to three feet tall.

Is blackberry lily easy to grow?

Yes. It will grow in just about any soil, withstands drought, and does best in full sun, although it tolerates light shade. It is readily propagated from seed.

Blackberry lily: The star-shaped flowers of blackberry lily are quite long-lasting.

Maggie Oster

Bishop's hat: This plant makes an excellent ground cover or rock garden plant.

Blanket flower *(Gaillardia)*

Can you suggest a bright-colored plant that will bloom continuously from late spring until fall? It must also tolerate drought and be easy to grow.

Gaillardia will certainly meet your needs. With showy red or yellow, or combination red and yellow flowers, gaillardia is readily grown from seed. The two- to three-foot-tall plants are long lived in dry, sandy, infertile soils with hot summers and full sun. Dwarf varieties need more moisture and a soil rich in organic matter.

Do *Gaillardias* make good cut flowers?

They are indispensable for the person who enjoys bouquets indoors. Naturally long-lasting, they last even longer if picked when the flowers are still slightly cup-shaped rather than fully open. The globe-shaped seed heads are also useful in fresh and dried arrangements.

When should I divide my *Gaillardias*?

In early spring, break up the old plants into several pieces.

How can I keep grubs out of the stems of *Gaillardias*?

Your grubs may be larvae of the common stalk borer. The best control depends on cleaning up all weeds and woody stems in autumn. Serious infestations can be controlled with a spray of methoxychlor-Kelthane mixture in late June; repeat twice at ten-day intervals.

Bleeding-heart (*Dicentra*)

What are the cultural requirements of bleeding-hearts?

Most do best in light shade, although in cool climates they will grow in full sun. If planted in too deep shade, they will not bloom. Provide a rich, light, well-drained but moist soil. Propagate from seeds, plant division, or stem or root cuttings. Division should be made in September. Transplant in early autumn or early spring.

I mulched a large bleeding-heart with leaves last winter, and yet it died. What might have been the cause?

You may have used too many leaves and smothered the plant; or perhaps you covered it too early. Wait until the soil is frozen, then cover bleeding-heart plants lightly. Remove mulch gradually in the spring. It is also possible to lose bleeding-hearts because of mice eating the roots.

Blue plumbago, Bunge, Leadwort (*Ceratostigma*)

My flower border doesn't seem to have much color in late summer. Can you suggest a low-growing plant as an edging in the front of my sunny border?

Blue plumbago would be a good choice, with its cobalt-blue flowers from midsummer until frost. The foot-tall mass of dark green leaves turns reddish-bronze in autumn. With protection, it is hardy to -20° F. Plants grow in any good garden soil and can be propagated by dividing the roots in spring.

Blue stars, Amsonia (*Amsonia*)

Can you tell me the name of a lovely blue-flowered perennial in my neighbor's garden? It has willowlike foliage and bears clusters of clear blue, star-shaped flowers in midspring. Its height is about three feet.

You are probably describing blue stars or willow amsonia. It is native to much of the upper South and as far west as Texas, but it is also quite hardy in northern gardens. It does well in partial shade. Propagate by seeds or by division in spring or fall.

Boneset. See Mist flower.

SELECTED BLEEDING-HEART

Japanese bleeding-heart *(D. spectabilis)* grows two to four feet tall, with thin, blue-green, fernlike leaves. It blooms in spring with sprays of heart-shaped, rosy crimson or white flowers. It is hardy to -50° F.

Eastern bleeding-heart *(D. eximia)* grows twelve to eighteen inches tall, with handsome gray-green, finely divided leaves topped with sprays of small pink or white flowers in early spring and again in fall. In cool climates, flowering continues off and on all summer. Plants readily self-sow. It is hardy to -40° F.

Pacific bleeding-heart *(D. formosa)* grows to twelve inches tall, with small pink or white flowers. Plants may spread rapidly from root growth. It is hardy to -40° F.

Bugbane, Snakeroot *(Cimicifuga)*

Will bugbane naturalize in a moist, shaded area of my yard?

This is an ideal location, particularly if the soil is rich in organic matter. Propagate by division of the plant or by seeds sown as soon as they are ripe.

Will bugbane spread and become a pest if I plant it in my flower border?

No. Although it readily naturalizes, it will not get out of control. It is a very elegant plant for the back of the border. The blooms are lovely in bouquets, too.

Why might the bugbane that I planted last year not have bloomed?

Bugbanes need to be established for several years before giving the normal display of bloom.

Bugleweed *(Ajuga)*

What ground cover do you suggest for an area that has both sun and light shade?

Bugleweed *(A. reptans)* will quickly form a thick mat either in sun or shade in just about any soil, and it is hardy to -40° F. Its leaves are evergreen in mild climates. Space the ground-hugging plants six inches apart for quick cover. Propagate by division or from seed.

Bugloss *(Anchusa)*

Can you suggest a tall-growing, deep blue-flowered perennial for planting in masses in either full sun or partial shade?

Try perennial bugloss, which bears large, loose clusters of forget-me-not-like flowers in June and July. Extend the blooming season by removing the faded flower sprays.

Will you please give the cultural care of bugloss?

Good, moist but well-drained garden loam and division every three years. Bugloss also readily self-sows.

Bunge. See Blue plumbago.

Butterfly flower, Milkweed *(Asclepias)*

Butterfly flower is so beautiful in the fields and along roadsides. Can it also be grown in the garden?

Certainly. Even with dry soil and competition from grass, it produces masses of brilliant orange flowers on two- to three-foot

Maggie Oster

Bleeding-heart: This old-fashioned favorite does well in light shade in most areas.

stems during the hottest part of summer. Best of all, it attracts hordes of butterflies with its sweet nectar. Hardy to -40° F., it requires full sun and well-drained soil. Propagate by seed; division is possible but difficult due to deep roots.

Campion, Catchfly, Maltese cross *(Lychnis)*

How do I grow Maltese cross?

Lychnis chalcedonica grows two to three feet tall and bears clusters of brilliant orange-scarlet flowers in midsummer; it will continue to bloom if faded flowers are removed. Hardy to -40° F., it is long lived and easy to grow in either full sun or light shade, and well-drained soil. Propagate by seed or division.

Can you describe rose campion?

Rose campion has downy, silver-gray stems and leaves, and striking cerise, white, or cerise-eyed flowers on twenty-four- to thirty-inch plants. It self-sows readily and seedlings reach flowering size in a year, but plants are short lived. Provide full sun and well-drained soil. Cut off faded flowers.

How did catchfly get its name? How do I grow it?

The common name of *L. Viscaria* comes from the sticky stems just below the flowers. Tufts of grasslike foliage grow twelve inches tall and bear fragrant magenta flowers in midsummer. Hardy to -40° F., plants grow in full sun and well-drained soil. Propagate by division or seed.

Candytuft *(Iberis)*

Will you give me directions for the proper culture of candytuft?

Hardy to -40° F., candytuft, a tough little evergreen, usually grows satisfactorily in full sun or partial shade, in any well-drained garden soil that is not too acid. A good edging or rock garden plant, it should be cut back to within a couple of inches of the crown after it has flowered.

How can I propagate candytuft?

By seeds sown in the spring; by dividing the old plants in autumn or spring; or in the summer, by cuttings made of the young growth inserted in a cold frame.

Why does candytuft turn white and appear to die? It looks like mildew.

White rust is common on candytuft. It appears as white pustules on the underside of the leaves, which turn pale. Destroy diseased plants or plant parts, and dig out any cruciferous weeds, such as wild mustard. Spraying with bordeaux mixture may help.

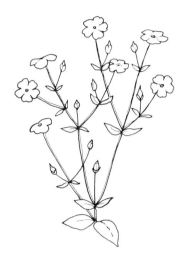

Rose campion: The self-sown seedlings of rose campion usually flower within a year.

Ann Reilly

Candytuft: A tough little evergreen, candytuft may be grown in either full sun or partial shade.

Canterbury-bells. See Bellflower.

Cardinal flower. See Lobelia.

Carnations, Hardy pinks, Sweet william *(Dianthus)*

Which of the hardy pinks do you recommend?

The most reliable of the garden pinks is cottage pink *(D. plumarius)*. Hardy to -40° F., this low-growing plant with gray-green, grasslike leaves has very fragrant, clove-scented flowers, in colors ranging from white to bright scarlet.

Is sweet william related to the hardy pinks? Is it a biennial or a perennial?

Yes, sweet william *(D. barbatus)* is one of the pinks and it is a biennial, but in cool climates it may live three or more years. It so readily self-sows, furthermore, that once it is established, you will seldom ever need to start new plants. In midsummer, the brilliant clustered blooms of sweet williams range in color from white to very dark red. Sweet william grows twelve to eighteen inches tall, although there are some very dwarf varieties.

Maggie Oster

Although technically a biennial, colorful sweet william readily self-sows and thus, once established, comes back year after year in many gardens.

What are some of the ways to use pinks in my garden?

Freely blooming pinks make good cut flowers, and are well suited for rock gardens, flower borders, or anywhere an edging is wanted.

After several years in my garden, my double pinks are all singles. What happened?

Pinks readily self-sow. Double types do not come true from seed, but the singles do.

How should I plant and care for hardy carnations?

Sow seeds indoors in March in a sterile, soilless mix. After seeds have germinated, transplant the seedlings into flats, 2 inches apart, or into peat pots. In May, prepare the outdoor bed, which should have well-drained soil and full sun. Fork in leaf mold or peat moss, and add about ten pounds of dehydrated cow or sheep manure per 100 square feet. Place plants about twelve inches apart. Water after planting. When seedlings are six to eight inches tall, pinch out the tips to induce branching. Cultivate the soil around the plants to keep it loose until the end of June, then mulch with old leaves or compost. Keep the plants watered. Disbud side shoots to encourage larger blooms on the main stem. Because carnations flower best in cool weather, keep buds removed until late summer.

The foliage of my pinks turns brown in the center of the clump and then spreads until the entire plant is dead. What is wrong?

It may be a fungus stem rot, which can be partially controlled by spraying with captan, or move healthy plants to a new location in very well-drained soil.

What is wrong with my hardy carnations? I get them started and they bloom until August, then droop and die.

Perhaps your carnations dry out. Try adding more organic matter to the soil to help retain the moisture. Or, the weather may be too hot and humid where you live.

Carolina lupine *(Thermopsis)*

What is the plant that looks like lupine, with its three- to five-foot-tall, bright yellow flowers in midsummer?

This is Carolina lupine, which is hardy to -40° F. It will grow in any deep, well-drained soil, is drought tolerant, and needs full sun. Divide the plants in spring or sow seed outdoors as soon as it ripens in the fall.

Catchfly. See Campion.

Catmint *(Nepeta)*

I recently visited a garden with a path edged in a plant labelled catmint. The bushy plants were about eighteen inches tall, with small, silver-gray leaves and sprays of tiny blue flowers. Can you tell me more about this plant?

Related to catnip, catmint is hardy to -40° F., and does well in sun in any well-drained soil. Blooming first in early summer, it will bloom again if the faded flowers are removed. Besides an edging to paths, catmint is also excellent in the front of the flower border, around beds of roses, or combined with pink flowers.

Chinese forget-me-not, Hound's-tongue *(Cynoglossum)*

I have average garden soil. Will Chinese forget-me-not grow successfully?

These two-foot plants do best in most soils, as long as they are well drained. Choose a site in full sun. Propagate by division in the spring or root cuttings in the fall. It is hardy to at least -20° F. Masses of rich, gentian-blue flowers, one-half inch across, are borne in July and August.

Chinese-lantern *(Physalis)*

The unusual, bright orange husks of Chinese-lantern are so wonderful for dried arrangements. Are the plants hard to grow?

Actually, Chinese-lantern is so easily grown in most soils that it can become a weed if the seeds are allowed to drop. It needs full sun. Plants grow thirty inches tall and are hardy to -40° F.

Cholla. See Prickly pear.

Christmas rose, Lenten rose *(Helleborus)*

Which of the hellebores is easiest to grow?

The Lenten rose. Growing eighteen inches tall, hybrid varieties provide a range of color from cream to pink, maroon, and green, with some spotted or streaked. Each stem bears several flowers that last up to three months. Plants self-sow and naturalize readily. It is hardy to -30° F.

How should I establish Christmas and Lenten roses?

Select a position in partial shade where the soil is rich and moist; add well-rotted manure, peat moss, compost, or leaf mold. Obtain young plants from local or mail-order sources and set them out in early spring. Do not allow plants to dry out during the summer.

Chinese-lantern: Bright orange Chinese-lantern plant readily self-sows.

Maggie Oster

Lenten rose: Like Christmas roses,
Lenten roses do best in partial shade,
in rich, moist soil.

What does the Christmas rose look like and when does it bloom?

The two-inch flowers have five white petals and golden stamens in the center; sometimes the petals are flushed with pink. Flowering occurs whenever temperatures are above 15° F. It is hardy to -40° F.

I have a Christmas rose that I have had for three or four years, and last year was the first it bloomed. Now I would like to move it. Will that set it back again three or four years?

Unfortunately, it may, for the Christmas rose does not like to be disturbed. Moving it carefully with a very large soil ball helps, but it is best to leave it in place.

Will you tell me how to divide hellebores? Mine are doing wonderfully well, but I would like to give some away.

It is best to divide them in late summer or autumn by taking a spading fork and lifting the side shoots without disturbing the main plant.

Chrysanthemum *(Chrysanthemum)*

I think of chrysanthemums as fall flowers. Is this so?

Chrysanthemums in the garden give a profusion of bloom in bright autumn colors as a grand finale to the gardening season.

70

Light frosts do little damage to either the flowers or foliage. If planted in protected spots, they will often remain attractive until mid-November in the latitude of New York state. Farther south, and in other milder climates, they are even better adapted, and a much larger selection of varieties can be used. Most will survive to -30° F. with some winter protection.

What are some tips to get chrysanthemums to bloom freely?

Choose a sunny location. Don't crowd them together or among other plants. Spade the soil deeply. Add a complete general-purpose garden fertilizer, plus a three- to four-inch layer of compost or other form of humus, to the soil under your plants. Cultivate frequently but lightly, and water copiously when needed. Divide plants every other year.

What type of soil is best for hardy chrysanthemums?

Any loose, crumbly soil is satisfactory. It should be well drained yet reasonably retentive of moisture. If the subsoil is heavy clay, improve its texture by adding manure, compost, leaf mold, or peat moss in the fall. Chrysanthemums will not succeed in waterlogged soil. They prefer soil with a pH 6 to 7, or slightly acidic.

Should hardy chrysanthemums be fed during the summer?

Apply a light dressing of a complete fertilizer, such as 5-10-10, into the soil around the plants when they are half grown. A liquid fertilizer applied in late summer or early fall works wonders, too.

When should one plant chrysanthemums?

Small plants are usually set out in the spring, but potted plants or plants with a large root ball can be set out any time during the growing season.

What is the best way to plant bare-root chrysanthemums?

With a trowel or spade, make a hole of ample size to accommodate roots. Set the plant in position so that the crown (the place where stem and roots merge) will be at soil level. Spread out the roots, and work the soil in among them, pressing the soil firmly with your fingers so that no air pockets remain. Do not plant chrysanthemums when the soil is wet and sticky. Water after planting.

How can I grow many-branched chrysanthemums?

Keep plants young by frequent division (see below), and pinch them back two or three times during the growing season—first when they are nine to twelve inches high, then when they are about fifteen inches high, and possibly a third time in late July. Cut back all strong shoots. A simpler way is to top the plants with a garden shears. Cushion-type varieties require no pinching. The shoots that you remove can be rooted.

What is the best way to care for chrysanthemums after they stop blooming in the fall?

Cut the stems back close to the ground. If brown foliage appeared during the summer, burn the stems and all dropped leaves—they may harbor insects or diseases. Cover plants lightly with evergreen branches and dry leaves when the soil is slightly frozen, after the first killing frost.

How should I care for hardy chrysanthemums in the spring?

Divide strong-growing kinds every year, and moderate-growing, every second year. When the shoots are three to four inches high, dig up the clump, and discard the old center portion. Separate the young offshoots, planting them singly, ten to twelve inches apart in well-prepared soil. If possible, give them a different location. Otherwise, fork some manure, compost, or fertilizer into the surface soil.

Can hardy chrysanthemums be moved when in bloom?

Yes. Be sure the soil is moist, then take up the clump of soil with a good root ball and replant immediately, firming the soil around the roots. Shade for two or three days, and don't neglect watering.

Why didn't my hardy chrysanthemums bloom this year? The leaves became gray.

Evidently the plants were badly mildewed. Do not crowd plants and be sure they have plenty of sun.

What causes the leaves of chrysanthemum to curl up and turn brown?

This is the most common problem of chrysanthemums. Verticillium or fusarium wilt, septoria leaf spot, or improper watering will all turn foliage brown, but in nine cases out of ten, leaf nematodes are to blame.

About July something attacked my chrysanthemums; they broke off about three inches from the ground, leaving piles of what looked like white ant eggs. What caused this?

The stalk borer was probably responsible, and what appeared to be ant eggs was excrement from the caterpillar inside the stem. When you see borer injury, it is usually too late to help the plant. Cleaning up weeds, especially in the fall, is the best prevention.

What insect causes chrysanthemums to open only partially?

This may be the gall midge, which lives in little conical projections of the leaves and flowers. Pick off and destroy infested plant parts. A fungus disease, ray blight, also deforms flowers.

What is the small insect similar to a ladybug, but green with black spots, that eats the flowers, particularly the centers, of chrysanthemums every fall?

It is the spotted cucumber beetle. Control is difficult because sprays discolor the flowers. Pyrethrum or rotenone would be best. As a last resort, spray or dust with carbaryl (Sevin).

Cinquefoil *(Potentilla)*

I planted several different kinds of the perennial cinquefoil as an edging to my flower border and in a rock garden, and they all died. What was wrong?

Perennial cinquefoils are excellent plants in the right climate, but they do not like extreme heat and need winter protection in areas with minimum winter temperatures of -30° F. Soil should be rich in humus but well drained. Cinquefoil tolerates both sun and light shade. Thin them annually for best growth.

How are cinquefoil propagated?

The trailing stems readily root. These new young plants can then be lifted and transplanted.

Columbine *(Aquilegia)*

My columbines never grow into healthy plants, although they have full sun and the other plants around them grow very well. Why?

Almost any location, except a hot, dry, windy one is suitable for columbine, although some light shade is beneficial. They need a well-drained, sandy loam that is neutral or slightly acid. Prepare the ground at least a foot deep and incorporate a two-inch layer of rotted manure, peat moss, or rich compost. Space the plants at least nine inches apart. Do not plant them too deep or the crown will rot.

How should I divide columbines?

Dig up the clumps, shake off the soil, and gently pull the plant apart, taking care to keep the roots from being broken.

What remedy will prevent crown rot?

Crown rot is caused by *Sclerotium rolfsii,* a fungus that is generally prevalent in the soil and attacks many different plants.

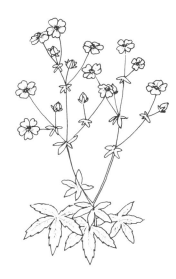

Cinquefoil: Provide winter protection for cinquefoil where winter temperatures drop to -30° F.

Columbine: Keep these graceful plants out of hot, windy, dry locations.

Maggie Oster

Leafminers make serpentine trails in the leaves of such plants as columbine.

Soil sterilization is difficult and not too satisfactory. The best treatment is to remove infected plants as soon as they are noticed.

The leaves of our columbine have little silvery-white lines all over them. Could you tell me the cause?

These are the serpentine tunnels of the columbine leaf miner. The larvae work inside the leaf and a small fly emerges to lay eggs for the next generation. Although this does not kill or even damage the plant, it is unsightly. There is no cure, but picking off and burning all infested leaves as soon as they are noticed, and cultivating the ground around the plants in the fall and early spring, will help prevent further infestations. Spraying with Orthene or malathion may help.

How can one keep the roots of columbine from becoming infested with worms?

The worms are probably millipedes, which usually swarm around when a plant is weakened or dead from other causes, either disease or unfavorable cultural conditions. They cause little injury, but can be controlled with either diazinon or malathion.

I lost hybrid columbines in a perennial bed where everything else thrived. What might have caused this?

Hybrid columbines, like hybrid delphiniums, are usually short lived. Your sudden loss, however, may be due to a fungus disease called crown rot, or to the columbine borer.

How can I fight columbine borer?

This is a salmon-colored caterpillar that works in the crown of the plant. All you can do is pull up and discard the infected plant, and in the fall destroy all weeds and other debris that might harbor borer eggs during the winter. Protect other columbines by spraying with Sevin.

What causes my columbine plants to turn brown?

This is probably due to spider mite, a tiny mite that makes webs on the underside of the leaves. Spray with Kelthane or insecticidal soap.

Coneflower, Gloriosa daisy *(Rudbeckia)*

What are the uses of coneflowers?

The bright yellow flowers of coneflowers in mid- to late summer are glorious—and they make lovely cut flowers. They are excellent for planting in large drifts (informally shaped groups) or meadow gardens. Most varieties survive minimum winter temperatures of -40° F.

What kinds of soil and light are best for coneflowers?

They will flourish in any reasonably fertile soil that is neither too wet nor too dry and receives full sun. Divide them every four years, or more frequently if plants are spreading quickly.

Coralbells *(Heuchera)*

Coralbells are so graceful. What are the growing requirements?

The low-growing clumps of leaves, marked by eighteen- to twenty-four-inch spikes of delicate coral-pink flowers in spring and summer, have made coralbells a favorite of gardeners and anyone who loves to bring bouquets of flowers indoors. They are easily grown in moist, rich, well-drained loam, in full sun or light shade. They are hardy to -40° F. The red-flowered types attract butterflies. Cutting off the spent stems of coralbells will cause flowers to be produced through summer, especially in areas with cool summer temperatures.

When and how do I divide coralbells?

Coralbells need division only about every three or four years, particularly if mulched. Take up clumps in early spring or fall, and break them into pieces with as much root attached as possible. Replant about twelve inches apart.

Cowslip. See Marsh marigold.

Cranesbill *(Geranium)*

I thought geraniums were houseplants, but I'm told there are perennial garden varieties. Can you explain?

The common houseplant geranium is really a *Pelargonium.* The true *Geranium* species has both frost-tender and hardy varieties that grow twelve to eighteen inches tall, with flowers ranging in color from lilac to rosy purple. They flourish in most well-drained soils in areas with cool summers; but with light shade and moist soil, they will grow in hot-summer regions.

How are geraniums propagated?

They seldom need dividing, but if you want additional plants, push your fingers into the soil at the base of a plant and take out a piece with some stem and root, and replant it.

Cupid's-dart *(Catananche)*

What growing conditions does cupid's-dart need?

These plants need sun and sandy garden soil. Hardy to -20° F., cupid's-dart grows eighteen to twenty-four inches tall. The small blue flowers are useful for cutting, are everlasting, and are

Maggie Oster

Coralbells: Although the foliage of coralbells is ground-hugging, the tall, graceful flower stalks are light and airy and do not interfere with this garden sun dial.

produced all summer long. Cupid's-dart can be started from seed or propagated by division.

Dame's-rocket, Sweet rocket (*Hesperis*)

There was a lovely, sweet-scented plant with clusters of magenta-colored flowers in our garden when I was growing up. The plants were bushy, about three feet tall, and bloomed during summer. What might it have been?

You're describing an old-fashioned flower that is lovely for bouquets—dame's-rocket. There is also a white-flowered variety. Plants thrive in full sun or light shade in any good garden soil. They are grown from seed and readily self-sow.

My dame's-rocket has cabbage worms. How do I control them?

Spray your plant with *Bacillus thuringiensis*.

Daylily (*Hemerocallis*)

What accounts for the popularity of daylily?

Today's daylily is perhaps the perfect summer perennial. It is difficult to think of another perennial that requires so little care. The ribbonlike foliage is superb, remaining in good condition throughout the growing season. Although each lily-shaped flower lasts only a day, each stalk is so abundantly budded that the actual flower display goes on for weeks. There are thousands of varieties, with colors ranging from pale cream to soft yellow, bright yellow and gold, as well as apricot, pink, maroon, and almost fiery red. The clumps are vigorous and can be divided every few years, or, if they do not outgrow their space, they can be left indefinitely without disturbance. Many are deliciously fragrant. They are especially useful in informal landscape schemes and look well in the foreground of shrub groupings as well as in the flower border.

When is the best time to plant daylilies, and how should I do this?

Plant them in either spring or summer. They can be lifted even when they are in full bloom if a good clump of soil is taken and care is used not to damage the roots. Plants must be watered deeply and kept well watered for a week or two. Dig the soil deeply, adding well-rotted manure, leaf mold, peat moss, or compost. When planting, make the holes deep enough so that the roots are not crowded, and set the plants with their crowns just level with the soil.

Do daylilies have to be planted in the shade?

No. Daylilies will grow in full sun if the soil is rich and moist, but the more pastel varieties do best in light or partial shade.

Maggie Oster

Daylily: Dependable, vigorous, and often sweet-scented, daylilies are one of the best perennials to grow.

Why might daylilies fail to blossom?

Most commonly this is due to too-dense shade or over-crowded plants and exhausted soil.

How shall I divide daylilies?

They are sometimes hard to divide, especially old clumps. The best method is first to dig up clumps, then push two spading forks through the clump, back to back, and pry the clump apart. (See page 37.) Do not make the divisions too small if you want flowers the next year.

What is the main blooming season for daylilies?

July and August, although some bloom in June and others in September and October. The variety Stella D'Oro has become very popular for its long period of bloom, from May until early fall; flowers are two-and-one-half inches across and plants grow two feet tall.

When should I fertilize daylilies?

Feed them in late winter or in very early spring, then again in early fall, using a low-nitrogen blend such as 5-10-10.

Is there a daylily that is particularly fragrant?

Although many hybrids have some scent, the sentimental favorite is canary-yellow Hyperion, which blooms from July into August. Lemon lily *(H. Lilioasphodelus* var. *flava)* is also quite popular.

Delphinium, Larkspur *(Delphinium)*

How are delphiniums best used in the garden?

One of the most spectacular of garden flowers, most delphiniums are tall-growing and thus best used toward the back of a mixed flower border where they create strong vertical lines and accent points. However, lower-growing strains have been developed, which let you add the beautiful colors of delphiniums to other parts of the flower border.

In what colors are delphiniums available?

While the clear blue colors of delphinium are the most highly prized, sparkling whites, rich violets, and soft, pleasing mauves are also available. Two new dwarf varieties are quite vigorous: Blue Fountain and Magic Fountain. An old favorite, developed by the noted photographer Edward Steichen, is the bush-type Connecticut Yankee.

What are the climatic requirements of delphinium?

They are grown successfully throughout the United States and Canada.

Should a beginner buy delphinium plants or start them from seeds?

Either is satisfactory, but for quick results, buy plants. If you do decide to begin with seeds, sow them in well-prepared soil in a cold frame in August, in rows spaced about two inches apart, with seeds spaced about one-quarter inch apart. Cover with soil just so that the seeds are barely out of sight. Leave the seedlings in the frame during the winter and transplant them to the garden in the spring. Seeds may also be sown in the open ground if special care is taken to protect the young seedlings. Shade both the seedbed and young seedlings until plants are well developed. Alternatively, sow seeds indoors any time between February 1 and May 1. If started early enough (before April 1), many of the plants will bloom the first year, in late August or early September. As soon as the plants are big enough to handle conveniently, transplant seedlings to flats or individual peat pots containing commercial soilless mixture. The flats must have drainage holes. Grow them under fluorescent lights.

Can manure be used on delphiniums? What about other fertilizers?

Manure, if well rotted, is excellent. Mix it in when you prepare the soil or add it later as a topdressing. Apply about five bushels per 100 square feet. Delphiniums have a higher nitrogen requirement than almost any other garden flower. Unless the soil is already very rich, they should be fertilized at least twice a year with a complete commercial fertilizer such as 5-10-5. Make the first application in the spring when the new shoots are about four inches tall. A second application can be made about five weeks later.

Do delphiniums require lime?

They do best in a slightly acid soil (pH 6.8). Use lime only when a pH test indicates a pH of 6.5 or lower. If the soil is rich in organic matter, they will tolerate a much wider range of pH values (pH 5.5 to 7.2). Spread the lime evenly over the soil surface and work it into the top three or four inches.

Is there a way one can tell by observing the plants whether the soil is too "sweet" (alkaline) for delphiniums?

The leaves appear mottled with yellow or, in severe cases, with white. The veins usually retain their dark-green color.

How far apart should delphiniums be planted?

In perennial borders, plant them two to three feet apart; in cutting gardens give them more room—three to four feet between rows and two feet between the plants in rows.

When should delphiniums be transplanted?

Very early spring is best, if possible before growth starts. They can also be transplanted with success in the fall or immediately after their first period of bloom. Move them with a large ball of soil in order to disturb their roots as little as possible.

Can delphiniums be made to bloom in the fall as well as during their regular season?

Cut the flowering stems off as soon as possible after they have finished blooming. New shoots will then come up and flower in early fall.

How can a delphinium be staked?

When the plant is about three feet high, place three five-foot stakes in the form of a triangle around it. Tie a band of raffia or soft twine around the stakes about 1 foot above the ground. As

Maggie Oster

Delphinium: This spectacular flower has a higher nitrogen requirement than most other plants, so fertilize it at least twice a year.

the plant grows, tie additional bands around the stakes. If desired, individual stakes can be used for large-flowering spikes. This latter method is preferable in decorative plantings.

Do delphiniums need extra watering?

Delphiniums require large quantities of water, especially just prior to and during the flowering period. Water them thoroughly whenever the weather is dry as well.

Why have my delphiniums failed even though I moved them to a better spot and replanted them one foot from a hedge where they get southerly sun?

Probably the moving is responsible. They may do better as they become reestablished. However, you have set them too near the hedge. They should be at least two or three feet away. Keep them well fertilized and watered.

How can I prevent my delphiniums from growing tall and having brittle stems?

Vigorous delphiniums are likely to be brittle and break off during windstorms and rainstorms. Lack of nitrogen exacerbates the problem. Stake the plants adequately or buy lower-growing kinds.

Why do delphiniums freeze in the winter?

Delphiniums are really very hardy plants, seldom killed by low temperatures. They are more likely to be smothered by snow, ice, or poor drainage. Diseases, especially crown rot, can develop during the fall, winter, or early spring, and kill the plants. Heaving is another hazard. Freezing and thawing action can cause shallow-rooted delphiniums to be heaved out of the ground, exposing them to the air and cutting off their ability to absorb vitamins and moisture from the soil. Some leading growers consider the English strains hardier than the American strains, which were developed on the Pacific coast.

Should young, fall-planted delphiniums be mulched?

It is always a good idea to give seedlings transplanted in the fall protection from heaving by mulching them lightly with marsh hay or straw. In areas with very cold winters, give them extra protection by keeping them in a cold frame, covered by a window sash to keep out snow and rain.

Can delphiniums be grown in areas with warm climates, such as Florida?

Grow them as annuals by sowing seeds early each spring. The plants are not usually successfully carried over a second year. In fact, delphiniums live longer in regions where summers are fairly cool. Hot, muggy weather is not to their liking.

Is it wise to divide delphiniums that have grown to a large size?

Yes. Lift the plants, shake off the soil, and cut the clumps apart with a strong knife. Replant them immediately in well-prepared soil. Each division should contain three to five shoots.

Why do my delphiniums get a black rot after one period of bloom?

Rotting is usually worse in wet weather and with succulent tissue. Some growers feel that the act of cutting down the old stalks after they bloom actually spreads the rot organisms.

How do you control black spot on delphinium?

This bacterial disease appears as tarlike black spots on the leaves. It is not serious except in wet seasons, when it may be controlled by spraying with bordeaux mixture. In a normal season, picking off infected leaves and cleaning up old stalks in autumn should be sufficient.

Is there a remedy when leaves curl and the plants fail to bloom, or when they have green blossoms?

This is probably aster yellows, a virus disease carried by leafhoppers. There is no cure except taking out infected plants as soon as you notice them and spraying the plants with contact insecticides to control the leafhoppers. Such diseases are common in the Northwest.

Is mildew on delphiniums caused by the soil?

No. Mildew is a fungus disease that infects the leaves. It is seldom serious before late summer. It can be controlled by spraying the plants with Benlate or Karathane or by dusting with sulfur. Prevent mildew by giving plants adequate spacing, using mildew-resistant strains, and cleaning up old plant material.

What causes the yellowing of leaves on hybrids?

Your plants may need nutrients, especially nitrogen. Apply fertilizer every ten days, but be careful not to apply too much; getting too succulent a growth will mean more rot diseases. Yellowing might also be due to fusarium wilt, a fungus common in soils in the Middle West. In this case, there is usually a progressive yellowing of leaves from the base upward. The yellowing may also be due to crown rot, lack of water, or intense heat. Try a new location.

My delphiniums are deformed, stunted, and marked with black streaks and blotches. What is wrong?

Your plants are infested by an exceedingly minute, common, and serious pest—the cyclamen mite. This light-colored relative

Delphinium and desert-candle: The varying heights of tall desert-candle and delphinium contrasted with Oriental poppies make a striking display.

Maggie Oster

of the spider mite is too small to see with the naked eye. It deforms the leaves, blackens the flower buds, usually preventing bloom, and stunts the plant. Cut off and destroy badly infested shoots. Spray every ten days from early spring to flowering time with Kelthane or insecticidal soap. Pick off any deformed plant parts, and discard severely infested plants. Avoid planting delphiniums near strawberries, which are also host to this mite.

What should be done for brown spots on the underside of delphinium leaves?

If these spots are rather glassy in appearance, they are due to the broad mite, which is not as harmful as the cyclamen mite and is more readily controlled with sulfur dust.

What causes blighted areas in the leaves?

The larvae of leafminers feed inside the leaves, which collapse and turn brown over rather large areas, usually near the points. Remove infested leaves. Spraying with malathion may help.

Desert-candle *(Eremurus)*

What is the name of the plant that produces four- to six-foot-tall spikes of bell-shaped white, pink, yellow, or orange flowers in midsummer?

These are desert-candles. The white-flowered form is hardy to -30° F., while the other species are hardy only to -10° F. Although the flower spikes are tall, the wide, straplike leaves form a rosette, similar to yucca, only a foot or so tall.

My desert-candle comes up early and is sometimes damaged by frost. What can I do?

This is often a problem with desert-candle. If frost is imminent, cover each plant with a box, bucket, or pine boughs in the evening and uncover them the following morning.

What growing conditions are necessary in order to grow desert-candle successfully?

Desert-candles need deep, well-drained soil, protection from summer winds and from full sun, and a winter mulch in northern areas. Work some superphosphate into the soil each fall. Usually plants younger than four years old bloom little, if at all.

When is the best time to plant desert-candle?

Plant in the fall, since top growth begins early in the spring. Spread the roots out flat or they will snap off when being planted. Plant so that the crown is about two inches below the soil surface. Too-deep planting is apt to cause the crown to rot, especially in a heavy soil.

Can desert-candles be divided, and when?

They can be divided only with difficulty, unless they send up offsets (young shoots around their edges). Early fall is the best time to divide them. Be sure each division has a bud, or eye.

Evening primrose. See Sundrops.

False dragonhead *(Physostegia)*

How is false dragonhead best treated?

In late summer, false dragonhead bears spikes of tiny, snapdragonlike flowers that make excellent cut flowers. It is hardy to -30° F. and grows twenty-four to thirty-six inches tall, with flowers in many shades of pink and white. It does best in rather moist soil, particularly near streams or pools, in either full sun or light shade. Dig up and divide plants every two or three years.

False indigo *(Baptisia)*

I have had little success growing lupines, but I like the flower spikes so much. Is there any other plant with similar flowers?

Yes; try false indigo. The three- to four-foot plants bear twelve-inch-long spikes of blue flowers in midsummer. The foliage is gray-green. After the flowers fade, there are attractive seed pods. Hardy to -40° F., false indigo prefers full sun but tolerates light shade. It withstands dry, sandy soil, but does best in average garden soil. Propagate from seed or by division.

False starwort *(Boltonia)*

Can you recommend a white fall flower?

A false starwort called Snowbank resembles a hardy aster and blooms at the same time. Hardy to -40° F., it grows four feet tall. Plants tolerate a wide range of soils, as well as heat and humidity. Plant in a sunny location. Propagate by division.

Ferns

What growing conditions do ferns require?

Most ferns need slightly acid (pH 6.0 to 6.5) soil, rich in organic matter. Before planting, work a three- or four-inch layer of compost, leaf mold, decayed manure, or peat moss into the soil. The most critical factors to success are adequate shade and

False dragonhead: Plant false dragonhead in a moist area, such as by a pond or stream.

False indigo: This spiky flowering plant does best in full sun.

Maggie Oster

moist, but well-drained, soil. Propagate by division. All of the selected ferns (below) are readily available, easy to grow, and hardy to -40° F.

I have planted ferns under evergreens and they have not done well. Don't ferns need shade?

Sometimes the shade beneath evergreens is too dense even for ferns. Although it is possible to grow ferns under evergreens, the best location for them is beneath deciduous trees. Mass them along shady woodland paths, at the edges of pools and streams, or on the north side of the house.

What is wrong with a fern when it gets minute white and slightly larger brown specks all over it? The white ones can be moved, but the brown ones are tight.

This is a perfect description of fern scale. The white bodies are male; the brown, pear-shaped objects, female. A severe infestation ruins the fern. Remove badly infested fronds. Try spraying with malathion, using one-third the usual dosage; repeat three times at ten-day intervals and wash off with a pure water spray several hours later, as malathion injures ferns. Nicotine sulfate and soap will also clean up scale infestations.

SELECTED FERNS

The maidenhair fern (*Adiantum pedatum*) with beautiful, airy and graceful fronds, grows twelve to twenty-four inches tall and spreads slowly.

The lady fern (*Athyrium Filix-femina*) grows three feet tall with delicate, lacy fronds. With moist soil, it will tolerate full sun.

The Japanese painted fern (*Athyrium Goeringianum* Pictum) has two-foot, gray-green fronds marked with wine-red.

The hay-scented fern (*Dennstaedtia punctilobula*) is a rapidly growing variety that becomes invasive if planted in the wrong place, but given plenty of room, it is an excellent ground cover. Snails can mar the three-foot fronds; control them with slug bait.

The wood ferns (*Dryopteris* species) are excellent specimen plants, growing twenty-four to thirty inches tall with semi- to fully evergreen fronds, and are often used in flower arrangements.

The ostrich fern (*Matteuccia pensylvanica*) is one of the tallest of American ferns. Although they grow to ten feet in swampy areas, in most gardens four feet is the usual height. There are two types of fronds on the plants: the outer ones are lacy, while the stiff inner ones bear the spores. Plants spread by underground runners.

The sensitive fern (*Onoclea sensibilis*) is a rampant grower, whether in full sun or shade. The gray-green fronds are a markedly different color from that of most other ferns. Spore-bearing fronds are attractive in winter outdoors and provide fine material for dried-flower arrangements.

The cinnamon fern (*Osmunda cinnamomea*) is a bold plant with six-foot fronds. Although it needs constantly moist soil, it will tolerate full sun.

The royal fern (*Osmunda regalis* var. *spectabilis*) is another bold plant, also growing six feet tall. It requires very acid, moist soil. Both osmundas grow from a crown and spread slowly.

The common polypody fern (*Polypodium virginianum*) forms a low-growing, dense mat around rocks and fallen logs with moist soil and light shade. It is evergreen, even to -40° F.

The Christmas fern (*Polystichum acrostichoides*) resembles the Boston fern. Growing from crowns, the eighteen- to twenty-four-inch plants spread slowly. Fronds are semi- to fully evergreen.

What makes lacy holes in fern leaves? We can find no insect that causes it.

Possibly the Florida fern caterpillar, which feeds at night. It is about two inches long and varies from dark green to black. Spray plants and the soil surface with *Bacillus thuringiensis*.

Flax *(Linum)*

Are there any special requirements for growing perennial flax?

Perennial flax is a very undemanding plant, needing only full sun and well-drained soil. Plants may be propagated from seed or division, but, once established, they do not readily transplant. Winter protection may be needed at the northernmost limits of its hardiness.

Some days my flax does not bloom. Why is this?

Flax flowers will not open without sun. Also, flax has a tendency for the flowers to open only every other day.

Fleabane *(Erigeron)*

Does fleabane do well in most parts of the country?

In cool maritime climates, fleabane will flower all summer in full sun. In hotter climates, plants grow best in light shade and will flower for only a few weeks. Plant fleabane in a well-drained, sandy loam that is only moderately fertile. In the spring, propagate by division or sow seed. The pink to blue asterlike flowers are good for bouquets.

Foxglove *(Digitalis)*

Please describe foxglove and how to grow it.

Foxgloves bear spectacular, three- to six-foot-tall, white, lilac, purple, rose, and yellow flower spikes during midsummer. They do well in humus-rich, well-drained soil that is slightly acid. They grow in full sun if the ground is moist, and will readily naturalize in lightly shaded areas. Divide perennial foxglove in the spring.

Is there some way to get foxgloves to bloom a second time during the summer?

Yes. Cut off the main flower stem after it finishes blooming and other flowers will come up. Leave a few dead flowers on some of the plants to get them to self-sow and naturalize.

Should foxgloves be fertilized during the summer?

Yes. To get better blooms, feed them with a liquid fertilizer during flowering.

Maggie Oster

Lady fern: With its delicate, lacy fronds, lady fern tolerates full sun if the soil is moist.

Is a winter mulch necessary?

Most perennial varieties are hardy to -20° F., although in areas where temperatures typically drop that low, a light winter protection is beneficial. After a good freezing of the soil, apply a mulch of decayed leaves. Next, lay bare branches over the plants' crowns, and on top of this, spread an inch or two of marsh hay or straw. The branches serve to keep the covering from packing down on the crowns, thus causing rot. Evergreen boughs—not heavy ones—can also be used instead of the branch and straw combination.

What parts of foxglove are poisonous, if any?

Probably all parts. The drug digitalis (poisonous in overdoses) is obtained from the second year's young leaves.

Can you suggest some ways to use foxgloves in the landscape?

Plant them in masses among shrubs, in the flower border or along the edge of a woods or a brook. They are especially effective combined with pinks and sweet william.

Funkia. See Plantain lily.

Gas plant *(Dictamnus)*

How did gas plant get its name?

On hot, still summer days, a volatile oil builds up around the flower stalks. A lighted match placed near the flowers will give a flash of light from the gas as it actually ignites for an instant.

Is gas plant anything more than just a novelty?

Yes, it is actually a very beautiful, tough, long-lived perennial that is excellent both for the flower border and for cut flowers. The species has both white and pink forms, and blooms in early summer. Hardy to -40° F., the plants grow three feet tall. Leaves are a glossy, dark green with a faint lemony scent.

What are the growing requirements of gas plant?

They do best in a heavy, well-drained, rich soil in sun or partial shade. Once established, dry weather does not bother them. Plants do not respond well to transplanting, so let them stay where you plant them.

Gay-feather *(Liatris)*

What are the advantages of growing gay-feather?

These North American natives with grasslike leaves grow two to four feet tall, thrive in light soils, in sun or light shade, and are hardy to -40° F. Plants bear spikes of unusual, feathery purple or

Gas plant: A lighted match placed near gas plant flowers actually ignites the plant's volatile oil for an instant.

Maggie Oster

white flowers that are attractive to butterflies, excellent for cutting, and superb for drying. Propagate from seed sown in the fall, or by division of the tuberous roots.

Gentian *(Gentiana)*

No other flower color compares to the blue of gentian, but aren't they difficult to grow?

Try the less demanding crested gentian *(G. septemfida* var. *lagodechiana),* with deep-blue, bell-shaped flowers on plants six to twelve inches tall. Hardy to -40° F., it grows best in humus-rich, moist soil with light shade; it should be mulched. Divide in early spring.

Globeflower *(Trollius)*

The two-inch, buttercuplike blooms of globeflower are beautiful, but I've had difficulty growing the plants. Any suggestions?

The two-foot plants of globeflower *must* have humus-rich soil that is very moist but well drained, and light shade or full sun. They take several years to get established, but plants are hardy to -40° F. They may flower again after the main bloom of midsummer if faded flowers are removed.

How is globeflower propagated?

Because they are difficult to start from seed, globeflower plants should be divided. This is easily done, but it will be a while after division before they bloom again.

Globe thistle *(Echinops)*

A friend has an unusual plant that resembles a thistle, but I thought thistles were weeds. Can you tell me about this plant?

The globe thistle is neither a thistle nor a weed. It is a striking plant for the flower border, among shrubs, or as a bold specimen. About three feet tall, it has large, deeply cut, and very prickly leaves. Steel-blue, globe-shaped flowers, two inches across, bloom from June or July through September and attract bees.

Hardy to -40° F., globe thistle is very easy to grow, doing best in full sun and light soil. Plants seldom need dividing. They may be propagated from seed or by division.

How do I dry the flower heads of globe thistle?

Pick the flowers just before they open and hang them upside down in a cool, dry, dark, well-ventilated place to dry. The flowers may also be used in fresh arrangements.

Globeflower: Plant globeflower in humus-rich, very moist, but well-drained soil.

Globe thistle is a somewhat unusual and easy-to-grow blue-flowered perennial.

Maggie Oster

Maggie Oster

Goatsbeard: One of the best choices for wet spots, goatsbeard grows five to seven feet tall.

Goatsbeard *(Aruncus)*

What would you recommend for planting in a lightly shaded area along a small stream?

One of the best choices is goatsbeard. Hardy to -40° F., it grows five to seven feet tall. During summer, it produces spikes of feathery white flowers. If used in a perennial border, place it near the back and give it plenty of room. Clumps may be divided in spring, or start plants from seed.

Why is it that my goatsbeard never produces seed?

Goatsbeard has separate male and female plants. Yours must be a male plant, which does not produce seed.

Gloriosa daisy. See Coneflower.

Golden marguerite *(Anthemis)*

What is the plant with yellow, daisylike flowers and grayish, finely divided leaves that grows in poor, dry soil?

You're probably thinking of golden marguerite. The flowers, excellent for cutting, are two inches across, and plants grow two to three feet tall. They are hardy to -40° F. They flower best in full sun, but tolerate light shade. Plant them in masses; they grow and spread rapidly. Propagation is easy by seed or division.

Goldenrod *(Solidago)*

Won't goldenrod in the garden give me hayfever?

Contrary to popular belief, ragweed, which blooms at the same time, is the culprit, not goldenrod. Hybrids produce large sprays of golden yellow flowers in late summer. Easy to grow in any soil, they are a worthwhile addition to the garden. They do best in full sun, but tolerate light shade. They are hardy to -30° F.

How is goldenrod propagated?

Although goldenrod can be started from seed, cultivars should be propagated only by division.

Goldentuft. See Basket-of-gold.

Goutweed. See Snow-on-the-mountain.

Greek valerian, Jacob's-ladder *(Polemonium)*

What is the plant with fernlike foliage and blue or white flowers?

You are probably referring to the *Polemoniums,* Greek valerian or Jacob's-ladder. They prefer humus-rich, dry soil with light shade, and are hardy to -40° F. Sow seed in the fall or divide the plants in early spring.

Hardy aster, Michaelmas daisy *(Aster)*

What are the pink or purple, daisylike flowers growing along the roadside in the fall? Can they be grown in the garden?

These beautiful native plants are asters. Over the years, different ones of these have been selected and hybridized into some of our best garden plants. Most varieties grow three to six feet tall. New England asters *(A. novae-angliae)* and New York asters *(A. novi-belgii)* are both hardy to -30° F.

Are there any special tips for growing asters?

Asters tolerate a wide range of soils, though New England asters are more tolerant of wet soil. They do best with plenty of water during the growing season, but they must never have "wet feet" during the winter. Choose a site with full sun, and plant them in the spring, before they have more than an inch or two of growth. Pinch them back in early summer to encourage bushiness.

Greek valerian: Sometimes called Jacob's-ladder, this plant needs a relatively dry soil and light shade.

What are some ways to use asters in the landscape?

Plant them in large, informally shaped groups, called drifts. The taller types make a fine background for lower perennials, or use them in front of evergreens, along the edges of woodlands or roadsides, to soften a fence, and in the perennial border. They are excellent flowers for cutting.

How can I prevent my asters from getting a white powdery substance on the leaves?

This mildew can usually be prevented by keeping the soil moist during the growing season.

My asters bloom well, but the plants often "open up" in the middle. What should I do?

Asters have this tendency to open up as the plants age. Divide them at least every two years in the spring, thus maintaining only young plants in your garden. They multiply rapidly and there are always some to share.

Hardy begonia *(Begonia)*

Is there really a begonia that can be grown and overwintered outdoors in the north?

Begonia grandis (B. Evansiana), with red-veined, wing-shaped leaves and pink flowers, is hardy to -10° F., if it is mulched. It must have moist but well-drained, humus-rich soil and partial shade. Many gardeners in the South plant it among azaleas and camellias.

Hardy fuchsia *(Fuchsia)*

The unusual, pendulous flowers of fuchsia are my favorites. Is there a type that is hardy?

In areas with a winter minimum of 0° F., *Fuchsia magellanica* can be grown as a perennial. The three-foot-tall plant with dark green leaves bears red and violet flowers. It is often planted in rock gardens.

In what kind of light and soil should hardy fuchsia be planted?

Light shade and light, well-drained garden loam enriched with some leaf mold or other organic matter. Keep it out of exposed situations and try a light winter cover.

Hardy orchid *(Bletilla)*

Are there any orchids that can be grown outdoors but that do not require a lot of special care?

Bletilla striata is one of the easiest orchids to grow. Sprays of pink flowers appear in early summer. Lance-shaped leaves are a bright green. Provide moist, well-drained, humus-rich soil and partial shade. Plants grow twelve to eighteen inches tall. Propagate by division.

Hardy pinks. See Carnations.

Hen-and-chickens, Houseleek *(Sempervivum)*

How can I use ground-hugging hen-and-chickens in the garden?

Plant them among the paving stones of a terrace or path, in rock walls or gardens, or as an edging to a flower border. They like sandy, well-drained, fertile garden soil, with full sun, and are hardy to -30° F. To propagate, separate the offsets at any time of the year.

My hen-and-chickens died after it bloomed. What's wrong?

This usually happens, but because the plants produce so many offsets so quickly, it frequently goes unnoticed.

Offsets of hens-and-chickens may be dug up and replanted elsewhere.

Hollyhock *(Alcea)*

I thought hollyhocks were biennials, but my neighbor says she planted them only once and they bloom every year.

Although hollyhocks are officially biennials, they not only reseed readily but they also persist for a number of years. Hardy to -40° F., plants usually grow six to ten feet tall, though shorter varieties are available. There are both single- and double-flowering hollyhocks, in white, yellow, red, and pink. Plant them in full sun and deeply dug, humus-rich soil, and protect them from wind by planting them near a fence, wall, building, or hedge.

What causes the rusting, yellowing, and dropping of foliage of hollyhocks?

This is most likely fungus. Its spores are produced in little reddish pustules on the undersides of the leaves, while yellow areas appear on the upper surface. With a bad case of rust, the leaves turn yellow, wither, and fall off, and rust lesions can be seen on the stem as well as on the leaves. Remove infected leaves as soon as you see them. To prevent fungus, clean up all old stalks and leaves in the fall, and dust with sulfur and ferbam, starting in early spring. Be sure to coat the undersurface of the leaves.

Hound's-tongue. See Chinese forget-me-not.

Houseleek. See Hen-and-chickens.

Iris *(Iris)*

How are irises best used?

Iris comes in an array of sparkling hues and exquisite forms. Easy-care plants in a range of sizes and periods of bloom, irises

Iris reticulata*: This is one of the earliest irises to bloom, usually in March or April in a climate similar to that of New York City.*

Maggie Oster

are adaptable to many diverse uses in the landscape, such as in a mixed perennial border, but they are just as stunning when used as single accents by a wall or rock outcropping, for example. By themselves, they are not attractive during the greater part of the year. Clumps of one variety in front of evergreens are very effective. Many people interplant irises with daylilies. Irises are beautiful in bouquets, too.

How are irises classified?

There are both bulb and rhizome forms of iris. Among the bulbs are Dutch, Spanish, and English irises. Irises with rhizomes include both bearded and beardless irises, such as Siberian, Japanese, Louisiana, and crested.

Can you tell me the relative blooming times of the various irises?

Using the New York City area as a point of reference, you can anticipate blooms starting usually in March or April with *I. reticulata*, soon followed by the miniature, dwarf, and intermediate bearded irises in April and May. The tall-bearded and Siberian irises bloom in May and June, followed by Dutch, Louisiana, and Japanese in June and July. Some bearded irises bloom again in late July, August, and September.

Do irises grow better in sun or shade?

Most do best in full sun. Certain wild species, such as *I. cristata, I. gracilipes, I. verna,* and *I. foetidissima,* are satisfactory in partial shade.

Do irises grow better in low, moist ground or in dry soil?

Most irises need rich, well-drained loam. Bearded irises require sharp drainage. Beardless kinds, such as Japanese varieties, need plenty of moisture but not waterlogged soil; they should not be planted where water stands during winter. The yellow flag of Europe and our native *I. versicolor* and Louisiana irises succeed even in swamp conditions. Add bonemeal or superphosphate when making plant beds. If the soil is heavy, work in organic matter such as peat moss, leaf mold, or compost.

How should the soil be prepared for Japanese and Siberian irises?

These irises thrive in acid soil, or at least in soil that is not alkaline. Never apply lime, bonemeal, or wood ashes to Japanese irises. Siberian irises are more tolerant of alkaline soil, but prefer somewhat acid soil. Spade the bed deeply; incorporate plenty of humus—old rotted manure, leaf mold, peat moss, or compost. Also, if the soil is poor, spread on a thin layer of manure or general fertilizer.

What kind of soil is good for Dutch and other bulbous irises?

Any fertile, well-drained soil, other than heavy clay.

When, where, and how do you plant bearded irises?

The main planting period is in June or July after flowering to allow maximum time for recuperation before blooming the next year. They can also be planted in the spring and fall. Plant rhizomes level with the surface in well-drained, sunny beds in good garden soil. In light, sandy soil, the rhizomes can be covered an inch or so, but in heavy soils they should be left with the tops exposed.

When and how deep should Japanese irises be planted?

Plant them in early spring, before growth starts, or in late August. The crowns should be set two inches below the surface.

How should I plant Dutch, English, and Spanish irises?

Plant bulbs four to five inches deep, in October and November.

What distances should be allowed between irises when they are planted?

Tall-bearded, nine to eighteen inches; dwarf-bearded, six to nine inches; Japanese and Siberian, eighteen to twenty-four inches; bulbous, four to five inches. For the tall-bearded varieties, the shorter spacing will give a better effect the first year, but in the long run, the wider spacing is preferable.

Is manure good for irises?

Animal manure should not be used on bearded irises, but the beardless species (including the Japanese and Siberian irises) do better if well-rotted manure is applied. Dutch, English, and Spanish irises are heavy feeders and deplete the soil very quickly.

What fertilizer do you recommend for ordinary bearded irises?

When preparing the beds, mix into the soil a superphosphate fertilizer and unleached wood ashes (the nutrient value of wood ashes is quickly washed away by rain), together with a commercial fertilizer low in nitrogen. In subsequent springs, apply unleached wood ashes, which supply from five to twenty-five percent of iris's potash requirement, as well as thirty to thirty-five percent of the lime they need. Water the ashes in after applying about four to five ounces per square yard.

What is the best fertilizer to use on Japanese irises?

Apply rotted or dehydrated manure as a mulch in May or early June. If this is not available, use leaf mold or peat moss

Positive Images, Margaret Hensel

Iris: These bearded irises are best transplanted in June or July after the blooming period.

fortified with a light dressing of complete fertilizer, such as one formulated for rhododendrons and azaleas (acid-loving plants). In fall, mulch with manure, leaves, or peat moss.

How much watering and cultivating do irises need?

Bearded irises ordinarily need no watering. Japanese, Siberian, and other beardless types need plenty of moisture until their flowering is through. Cultivate them shallowly and often enough to keep the surface loose and free of weeds.

How often should I transplant irises?

Overcrowding will lead to lack of bloom. Whenever irises become so crowded that the rhizomes are growing over one another (about every three years), lift them and replant. Avoid moving bearded irises until after the blooming season or they may not bloom that year. Japanese and Siberian irises usually bloom even after being moved.

When should Dutch, English, and Spanish irises be transplanted?

Let them remain in place for two years, then lift them and replant them in a new location.

How are bulbous irises handled in the South?

To keep stalks from developing after bloom, Dutch, English, and Spanish irises should be dug up after flowering and stored in a cool shed until late fall, when they are replanted. If not removed from the ground in this manner, they make fall growth, and flower stalks are then usually killed by a freeze in late winter.

Do Dutch irises have to be dug up each year?

Not unless they have suffered winter losses other years. In that case, try planting as late in autumn as the weather permits. In extreme climates, a winter mulch is beneficial.

What care should be given bearded iris rhizomes after the blooming season?

If they become overcrowded, divide them. Remove the flower stalks immediately after flowering and be on the alert for signs of borer pests or rots. Keep all dead foliage cleaned off.

How and when should Japanese irises be divided?

This is quite a job if the clumps are large. A heavy-bladed knife is the best tool. Cut the leaves halfway back and then chop the rootstock into pieces, each with three or four growths. Save only young, vigorous portions, and discard old, lifeless material. Do this work in the shade, in the autumn or just before growth

Beautifully intricate irises are adaptable to many diverse uses in the landscape.

starts in the spring. Keep the roots from drying out during the process.

How should I divide tall bearded irises?

After flowering, cut the leaves back halfway, lift the clumps, then with a sharp knife cut the rhizomes into pieces so that each has one strong fan of leaves (or, if preferred, two or three) attached. Be sure that divisions are disease free before replanting them. Divide again every three or four years.

Does it injure iris plants to take green foliage off in the late fall?

Leaves turning brown should always be removed promptly. Green foliage should not be removed or cut back in late fall because this may adversely affect next year's bloom.

What can be used as winter protection for irises?

Bearded irises need no protection, unless their rhizomes have been planted in late fall. Evergreen boughs then make the best protection. Marsh hay or excelsior can also be used. Dutch, English, and Spanish irises benefit from mulch where winters are severe.

Why won't Japanese irises bloom for me?

There are several possibilities, including too much shade, alkaline soil, dry soil, and water settling around the crowns during the winter.

My bearded irises grow and look well, but rarely bloom. What is the reason? They have been established more than two years, and get full sun at least half the day.

Most likely they are overcrowded and need to be divided. Some varieties of tall-bearded irises require dividing every year for good bloom. And the more sun, the better.

My early dwarf and Siberian irises bloomed the first year but not the following two years. What is wrong?

Perhaps they do not get enough sunshine, or they may be too crowded and need to be divided. Siberians are heavy feeders; add superphosphate and lime, if necessary, to the soil.

How do you destroy the borers that attack iris?

The iris borer, a fat, fleshy-colored caterpillar with a dark head, is the major pest of irises. Sanitary measures are most important in getting rid of iris borers. Sometime in October or November, after a killing frost, clean up and burn all old leaves and debris where the moth lays its eggs. Leave only fans of new leaves. In the spring, start spraying new growth with malathion, pyrethrum, or rotenone, and repeat every two weeks. Kill young borers already in the leaves by squeezing leaf sheaths between your thumb and forefinger.

What causes brown spots on iris leaves?

This is fungus leaf spot disease. Cut back diseased foliage and burn it, or the disease will spread through the garden. Be sure to pick off dead leaves and clean up old leaves in the fall, and in two years you will have eliminated the disease. Leaves may also be dusted or sprayed with two or three applications of maneb or bordeaux mixture during summer. Avoid splashing water on leaves as this spreads the disease.

Are irises subject to virus diseases?

Iris mosaic disease attacks both bearded and bulbous kinds, causing mottling or yellow striping of leaves and lack of vigor. Destroy all infected plants.

Some of my iris rhizomes are rotting. Although the shell seems dry, the inside, if opened before destruction is complete, is wet and slimy. There are also watery streaks on the leaves. What is the cause?

Bacterial soft rot. The rot may start in the leaves, following puncture by young borers; there is often a water-soaked appearance to the leaves. Roots are slimy and vile-smelling. To control, first take measures against the borer (see above). Next, remove and immediately destroy any rotting rhizomes. Dig them out along with surrounding soil, and disinfect your trowel with a solution of one-half cup bleach mixed with one-half cup water. Sterilize the soil, as well as your knives and other tools that might spread the disease, by soaking them with the same mixture. A 70-percent denatured alcohol solution can also be used. Clean off and burn dead leaves and rubbish in the fall. When planting new irises, select a different area, and avoid planting diseased rhizomes.

Why do my iris blooms last only one or two days and die?

The life span of a single iris flower is only a day or two. On the other hand, if after one or two flowers bloom, the whole stalk withers and dies, a fungus disease may be working at the crown; or there may possibly be a very serious infestation of thrips.

Why do iris leaves turn brown and dry during July and August?

Crown or rhizome rot fungi may be the cause, or perhaps merely overcrowding and lack of water. If there are any signs of gray mold or white fungus threads with seedlike bodies around the base of the plant, remove and destroy infected rhizomes and the surrounding six inches of soil. Plant your iris in a different location.

Do you know anything about a little round beetle that destroys iris?

A small, round, flat, dark weevil eats iris pods and sometimes the petals. Try spraying with methoxychlor.

My beautiful iris garden is being ruined by root knot nematodes. What can I do?

The root knot nematode is one of the worst problems to irises in the South, since it cannot be killed by winter cold; furthermore, it is not readily starved because it thrives on so many different kinds of garden plants. If you have any land that has not been growing nematode-susceptible plants, you can start a new iris garden there with new rhizomes. If you must use the same location, you can take out the iris and have the soil professionally sterilized. Or, leave the remaining healthy plants in place and apply Nemagon.

Jacob's-ladder. See Greek valerian.

Japanese anemone. See Windflower.

Joe-Pye weed. See Mist flower.

Jupiter's-beard, Red valerian *(Centranthus)*

How should I treat Jupiter's-beard in my garden?

The two- to three-foot plants have gray-green foliage and small clusters of tiny fragrant flowers, which may be bright crimson to light pink. Hardy to -30° F., they do best in climates with cool summers. Cut off dead flowers to get a second blooming. Plants readily self-sow, or they may be propagated by division in spring.

Knapweed. See Perennial cornflower.

Lady's-mantle *(Alchemilla)*

What is the plant with pleated, gray-green, round leaves that often are marked with dew drops?

This is lady's-mantle, an easily grown plant reaching only twelve to eighteen inches tall and hardy to -40° F. It bears a mass of tiny, chartreuse-colored flowers in early summer, but it is grown mainly for its foliage.

Will lady's-mantle do well in partial shade?

In hot, dry areas, light shade is essential, but in cool, moist climates, full sun is tolerated. In either climate, rich, moist soil is necessary for best growth. Propagate it by division or seed.

Lady's-mantle: Although lady's-mantle bears small, chartreuse-colored flowers, it is grown mainly for its ruffled foliage.

Cindy McFarland

Lamb's ears. See Betony.

Larkspur. See Delphinium.

Lavender cotton (*Santolina*)

Can lavender cotton be used as an edging?

Yes. The gray foliage of lavender cotton and its rounded growth habit create a lovely formal edging to beds, borders, or paths. Plants also can be used in rock gardens. Hardy to -20° F., plants grow twelve inches tall. A dwarf form is six to eight inches high. Provide light, sandy soil, and full sun.

Leadwort. See Blue plumbago.

Lenten rose. See Christmas rose.

Leopard's-bane (*Doronicum*)

Most yellow, daisylike flowers bloom in the summer or fall. Are there any that blossom in spring?

Leopard's-bane is the earliest daisylike flower. Hardy to -40° F., it grows twelve to eighteen inches tall, with coarsely toothed, heart-shaped leaves and single, two-inch flowers. The flowers are excellent for cutting, but they do close at night.

My leopard's-bane disappeared during the summer. Is something wrong with it?

No, leopard's-bane frequently is dormant in the summer in hot climates. It is important to keep the soil moist where it is growing, even when it is dormant.

Leopard's-bane: These plants often go dormant during hot summers.

What is the best way to use leopard's-bane in my garden?

In climates with hot summers, leopard's-bane does best in light shade, otherwise it tolerates full sun. Plant it among tulips, daffodils, and other spring-flowering bulbs, in front of shrubs, or in the rock garden.

What are the growing requirements of leopard's-bane?

The shallow roots need cool, rich soil. Before planting, incorporate plenty of organic matter. Put a mulch around the plants to keep the soil cool and moist. Divide about every two years after flowering. Plants may also be started from seed.

Lily-of-the-valley (*Convallaria*)

Can lilies-of-the-valley be grown in an absolutely shady place?

Yes. They will grow in dense shade if the soil is fairly good, but will probably not bloom as freely as those in partial shade.

What are the soil and other growing requirements of lily-of-the-valley?

Plant lily-of-the-valley in the spring in moist, but not wet soil containing generous amounts of humus. Improve the soil before planting by spading in rotted manure, leaf mold, and peat moss. Each year in early spring, top-dress the bed with rotted manure, leaf mold, or compost. Do not allow the plants to become overcrowded.

Although my giant lilies-of-the-valley have splendid foliage, they produce only a few stems that bloom, and the plants don't multiply. What could be the trouble?

In very rich soil, the foliage will be good, but flowers will be scarce. After the plants are firmly established and the excess nutrients are used up, they should begin to bear more flowers.

Are the roots of lily-of-the-valley poisonous?

Yes. The drug convallaria, used in the pharmaceutical manufacture of a heart tonic, is made from lily-of-the-valley roots. The red berries that appear in fall are toxic, too.

Lily-turf *(Liriope)*

I've heard that some kinds of lily-turf are pests. Which ones are the best to grow?

Big blue lily-turf *(L. Muscari)* is an indispensable perennial ground cover in areas with minimum winter temperatures of -10° F. or warmer. Growing twelve to eighteen inches tall, the

Lily-turf: The arching, evergreen leaves of lily-turf make the plant particularly suitable for edging borders.

Maggie Oster

plants have arching, grass-like, evergreen leaves and flowers that resemble grape hyacinths. Group lily-turf plants at the front of the perennial border, plant them under and between shrubs, or use them to edge paths or as a ground cover around trees.

Does lily-turf need any special care?

Plants grow well in shade, in most well-drained soils. If leaves look shabby in the early spring, cut them way back. Propagate plants by division in early spring. Slugs and snails are their only pests.

Lobelia, Cardinal flower (Lobelia)

I have repeatedly tried to grow cardinal flower. Do you have any suggestions?

No native flower is as striking as the three- to four-foot, brilliant red spikes of lobelia—nor as maddening for the gardener. These plants naturally grow in wet places, such as swamps and streamsides, and they need afternoon shade. Although theoretically hardy to -40° F., in areas colder than -10° F. a winter mulch is recommended, but too much mulch may smother plants. No matter what you do, lobelia is naturally short lived, so plan on renewing the plant by replanting the new basal rosettes each year or by letting plants self-sow. You may have somewhat better luck with blue cardinal flower, which is less dependent upon moist soil for success.

Loosestrife (Lysimachia)

I love the bent spikes of white flowers on gooseneck loosestrife in midsummer. What kind of light and soil does it require?

The three-foot-tall loosestrife needs bright sun, though it will tolerate light shade in very hot areas. Soil should be moist but well drained. Propagate by dividing the roots in spring or fall. Loosestrife is hardy to -40° F.

Will yellow loosestrife become a pest in my garden?

The yellow flowers on leafy three-foot stems of *L. punctata* make it a bright addition to the early summer garden. In moist to wet soil and full sun, it will grow vigorously, but it should not become a nuisance if given plenty of room. Plants are hardy to -20° F. and will tolerate moderately dry soil with light shade.

Lungwort (Pulmonaria)

Is lungwort a good choice for growing in rich, moist soil in full or partial shade?

The spreading clumps of hairy, often spotted, leaves of lungwort grow twelve inches tall and are quite fine for the front of

Lungwort: These blue, pink or white blossoming plants are one of the first perennials to bloom in spring.

shady borders. Hardy to -30° F., they flower early in the spring with tiny, bell-shaped flowers of blue, pink, or white. Propagate by division in the fall.

Lupine *(Lupinus)*

Does lupine have any special soil requirements?

It needs a moist but well-drained loam. Incorporate leaf mold or peat moss when preparing the soil, and sprinkle well-rotted compost or a general garden fertilizer, such as 5-10-10, around established plants in early spring and again in summer. Most lupines do better in acid soil. Do not use lime around them.

Can lupines be transplanted?

Old plants do not readily survive being disturbed and are very hard to transplant. Young plants can be transplanted in very early spring if care is used to protect the roots. Lupines are short lived. For a constant supply, sow seed each year.

Mallow *(Malva)*

Are the mallows worth considering for the flower border?

These old-fashioned plants definitely add a lovely charm to the flower border. Easily grown, they do best with deep, moist, but well-drained, humus-rich soil, and full sun. For many weeks during midsummer they will bloom with white or variously shaded pink flowers that resemble single hollyhocks. Although short lived, they readily self-sow.

Maltese cross. See Campion.

Marsh marigold, Cowslip *(Caltha)*

What plant has bright golden, two-inch flowers and fresh green leaves in early spring, and grows along stream banks? Can it be grown in the garden?

Marsh marigold does best in very moist soil and shade, but adapts to average garden soil. Divide the plants in the spring.

Meadow rue *(Thalictrum)*

How can I use meadow rue in my garden?

The large, fluffy flower heads and columbinelike foliage of meadow rue add wonderful texture to the flower border. Provide a humus-rich, moist but well-drained soil. Plants need light shade in hot climates, but will take full sun in areas with cool summers. Propagate from seed or by division.

Ann Reilly

Lupine: Protect these showy plants against hot summer winds.

Meadowsweet, Queen-of-the-prairie *(Filipendula)*

Someone suggested a plant called queen-of-the-prairie for my garden. What is it like?

Queen-of-the-prairie, or meadowsweet, is a bold, dramatic plant that grows six feet tall, with feathery plumes of pink or white flowers from June to August. Hardy to -50° F., it is native to our meadows and prairies. To grow well, plants must have moist, humus-rich soil, and light shade. Some support may be necessary when plants are in bloom.

Michaelmas daisy. See Hardy aster.

Milkweed. See Butterfly flower.

Mist flower, Joe-Pye weed, Boneset *(Eupatorium)*

There is a beautiful flower similar to ageratum growing in fields near my house. What is it and would it be a weed in my garden?

The mist flower, or hardy ageratum *(E. coelestinum)*, is hardy to -10° F., and grows eighteen to twenty-four inches tall, with small, fluffy, azure-blue flowers in August and September. In sandy soils, it may spread too aggressively for a small garden, but in clay soils it makes a valuable addition to the flower garden. Plant it in full sun or light shade in moist but well-drained, average garden soil. Butterflies are attracted to the flowers, which are good for bouquets.

How deep should mist flower be planted?

The roots are stringy and shallow. Spread them out and cover them, about two inches deep, with soil. They are best moved in the spring before growth starts. Because they grow into quite a mat, which dies out in the center, they need to be lifted and transplanted every year or two.

One area of my garden has very wet soil. Is there a *Eupatorium* that will grow there?

Yes. The native plant known as Joe-Pye weed *(E. purpureum)* is excellent for naturalizing along woodland streams or in shady wet areas. Growing four to six feet tall, Joe-Pye weed has large, purple, showy heads of flowers in late summer and early autumn. Propagate from seed or division.

Monkshood *(Aconitum)*

Is it advisable to plant monkshood? I have heard that it is poisonous.

The roots of monkshood do contain poison. It is said to have been mistaken for horseradish on occasion and eaten with fatal

Maggie Oster

Joe-Pye weed: A native plant, Joe-Pye weed (Eupatorium purpureum) *is excellent for naturalizing in shady wet areas.*

results. With sensible precautions, there is no reason not to grow this stately plant with its spikes of blue, hoodlike flowers.

How can I best use monkshood in my garden?

Monkshood may be planted among shrubs or perennials in full sun to partial shade. It is especially effective with Madonna lilies, white phlox, and shasta daisies. The common monkshood (*A. Napellus*) has dark blue flowers in midsummer; azure monkshood (*A. Fischeri*) has lighter-colored flowers in late summer. Both grow three to five feet tall.

Does monkshood need winter protection?

It is hardy to -40° F., but it should be lightly mulched for the first and second winters after being planted.

How deep should I plant monkshood and in what kind of soil?

Plant it with the crown one inch under the surface, in rich, moist, well-drained, neutral to slightly acid soil. You can also sow fresh seed in late autumn.

How often should monkshood be divided?

These plants flower freely when they are in established clumps and can be left undisturbed for years.

Do you know why the glossy leaves of my monkshood might have turned black and diseased looking?

Hot, dry conditions can cause this. You may want to try moving it to partial shade. To do best, monkshood also needs plenty of moisture and a humus-rich soil.

Mountain bluet. See Perennial cornflower.

Mugwort. See Wormwood.

Orange sunflower *(Heliopsis)*

Where and in what type of soil should heliopsis be planted?

One of the best perennials for all-summer bloom, three- to four-foot-tall orange sunflower prefers full sun. Although it will grow in any garden soil, it will probably flower better in a fairly dry situation. It is hardy to -30° F.

Does orange sunflower require frequent division?

The plants are very vigorous, so they tend to become crowded after about three years, when they should be divided in early spring.

Maggie Oster

Monkshood: This old-fashioned, interesting flower can be left to flourish undisturbed for years.

Oriental poppy *(Papaver)*

Do poppies come in any color besides orange?

Yes. There are white, light and dark pink, deep red, and bi-color varieties. In addition, you can find a fine blood-red and a salmon-orange double.

Will you give full planting instructions and the care of Oriental poppies?

Plant poppies in August or September, or in early spring before growth starts. Oriental poppies dislike being moved, so be particularly careful to make the hole big enough so that the fleshy roots are not broken or twisted upward. Don't keep them out of the ground long. Water well if the weather is dry. A few weeks after being planted, a crown of leaves will appear. In relatively mild climates, these may remain green for part of the winter. To prevent crown rot, protect these plants in the winter with pine boughs or dry leaves.

Will Oriental poppies planted in the spring bloom the same year?

Yes, but only if you buy large, established plants. Plant them in March or early April, give them good care, and you are quite likely to get some flowers.

How shall I care for Oriental poppies?

They don't need much attention. Cut off the flowers as they wither. In the spring, work in a sidedressing of balanced fertilizer such as 5-10-5, but do not overfeed.

My Oriental poppies come up and grow well but never bloom. They get afternoon sun. Should they be in a different place?

Transplant in April or August into a sunnier spot.

After flowering, the leaves of my poppies start to turn yellow and then die. Is this normal?

Yes, poppies do lose their leaves, but new growth reappears in the fall. If you find them unsightly, plant something like daylilies nearby to hide them after they bloom.

Oriental poppy: These lovely flowers dislike being transplanted, but they grow well without much attention once established.

Ann Reilly

Ornamental Grasses

I'd like to learn more about ornamental grasses. Are they perennials or annuals and how can I use them in my garden?

There are both perennial and annual grasses for the garden. Most of the annuals are best grown for their flowers, which can be dried and used in arrangements. Perennial grasses can also be used this way, but they also add wonderful texture to the

Blue fescue: **Festuca ovina** *has stiff, silvery blue foliage that remains evergreen.*

SELECTED ORNAMENTAL GRASSES

The giant reed *(Arundo Donax)* grows six to twenty feet tall in moist, humus-rich deep soil. Hardy to 0° F., it bears leaves that are about two feet long and three inches wide. Red-brown flower plumes appear in late summer. Use among shrubs or as a specimen plant.

Feather reed grass *(Calamagrostis acutiflora* Stricta) produces a formal, vertical effect. Hardy to -20° F., it grows five to seven feet tall, with feathery blooms in midsummer.

Japanese sedge grass *(Carex Morrowii* var. *ex-pallida)* has gracefully swirling variegated leaves that form clumps twelve to twenty-four inches tall. Use in the flower border or as an edging. It is hardy to -20° F.

Pampas grass *(Cortaderia Selloana)* is probably the best known of the ornamental grasses, but it, too, is hardy only to 0° F. It forms spectacular ten-foot mounds of thin foliage and long, silky white plumes, and thus is often grown as an specimen plant. A pink-flowered form is also available.

Ravenna grass *(Erianthus ravennae)* resembles pampas grass but is not as showy. It forms large five- to ten-foot-tall clumps, and has arching, silvery leaves that bear long, thin spikes of silver-purple flowers. Hardy to -10° F., it is tolerant of light shade.

Blue fescue *(Festuca ovina* var. *glauca)* grows only ten inches tall and has stiff, silvery blue foliage. Hardy to -30° F., these plants are evergreen, but old leaves should be trimmed off in early spring. Plant in the flower border, or use in masses or as an edging.

Eulalia *(Miscanthus sinensis)* is possibly the best all-round, large-growing grass. Hardy to -30° F. with protection, it has a variety of forms. Plants grow five to seven feet tall, and in late summer they bear plumelike flowers.

Variegated purple moor grass *(Molinia caerulea* Variegata) produces dense, two-foot clumps of narrow, arching leaves. Flower spikes persist well into the winter. It is hardy to -30° F.

Fountain grass *(Pennisetum alopecuroides)* is very showy with its bristly, silver-rose, wheatlike spikes of flowers produced from mid- to late summer. Leaves are very slender, dark green, and arching. Plants grow three to four feet tall and are hardy to -20° F.

Giant feather grass *(Stipa gigantea)* grows six feet tall, with huge flower heads that change from green-purple to yellow. It is hardy to -20° F.

Ribbon grass *(Phalaris arundinacea* var. *picta)* grows two feet tall with green-and-white striped leaves. Very vigorous, it needs plenty of room to spread. It is hardy to -40° F.

Maggie Oster

Fountain grass: **Pennisetum alopecuroides** *bears its showy, wheatlike spikes from mid- to late summer.*

landscape. Depending on the species, these grasses and grasslike plants range in height from ten inches to twenty feet.

What are the cultural requirements of ornamental grasses?

Most grow well in full sun and any moist but well-drained soil. Other than those you want for arrangements, leave the flowers on the plant during the winter, then cut back plants to the ground in the spring. The most reliable way to propagate plants is by division.

Ornamental onion *(Allium)*

I enjoy both regular and Chinese chives but I don't want a separate herb garden. Can I plant chives among my flowers?

Most assuredly. Both regular chives, which grow twelve inches tall with pink flowers, and Chinese chives, which grow two to three feet tall with white flowers, are very decorative plants that add immeasurably to any flower border. Both can be used as cut flowers, too. Clump-forming, they can be lifted and divided like other perennials.

Pearly everlasting *(Anaphalis)*

Is there a gray-foliaged plant that does well in very moist soil?

A good choice would be pearly everlasting. It grows twelve to eighteen inches tall and is hardy to -40° F. In addition to its silvery leaves, pearly everlasting has heads of tiny white blooms resembling strawflowers. Plants are propagated by division.

How do I dry the flowers of pearly everlasting?

Cut the flower stalks when the centers of the flowers begin to show. Put the stems in a container of water for several hours, then hang them upside down in a dark, dry, well-ventilated area.

Penstemon. See Beard-tongue.

Peony *(Paeonia)*

What makes the peony such a popular perennial?

Hardiness, permanence, ease of culture, and freedom from pests are but a few of its merits. Diversity in flower form, attractive colors, clean habit of growth, and deep green foliage combine to produce a plant of exceptional value for mass plantings or for the mixed border. Peonies rank high as cut flowers because of their extraordinary keeping qualities. They do best in the North, for they require the low temperatures of winter to break the dormancy of the buds before spring growth will take place.

I planted peonies the last of November; was it too late?

Planting can be done any time until the ground freezes, but the ideal months are September and October. This gives plants an opportunity to become partially established before winter. It is possible, however, to move them in the spring as soon as the ground has thawed and replant them immediately. If you move them early enough, they will bloom the same year. Keep the soil moist at all times.

What type of soil is best for peonies?

Any rich, friable garden soil is satisfactory. Heavy clay soil should be well drained and improved by additions of organic material, such as well-rotted manure, peat moss, or leaf mold, to make it more loose and crumbly. Sandy soil, too, needs additions of organic matter, such as well-rotted manure or rich compost, as well as commercial fertilizer. In either case, use about four bushels of organic material per 100 square feet.

What is the proper method of preparing the soil for peonies?

Spade it to a depth of twelve to eighteen inches. Thoroughly work in the organic material and incorporate three pounds of superphosphate to each 100 square feet.

Do peonies need lime?

Peonies grow best in a slightly acid soil (pH 5.5 to 6.5). If the soil is very acid (below pH 5), apply lime at the rate of five pounds per 100 square feet several weeks before planting.

What kind and how much fertilizer should I use once my peonies are established?

Apply a commercial fertilizer such as 4-12-4 or 5-10-5 at the rate of four pounds per 100 square feet. Well-rotted manure is also satisfactory, but avoid the use of fresh manure.

How deep do peonies need to be planted?

The crown, from which the buds arise, should be only one to two inches below the soil level. If planted too shallowly, there is danger of the roots being heaved out during the winter before they become established. If planted too deep, however, peonies won't bloom for many years.

Is it necessary to dig up peony roots every year and break them up to obtain more blossoms?

No. It is best not to divide and transplant peonies any more often than is necessary to maintain vigorous growth, ordinarily, every five to eight years. Better quality blooms can be had by fertilizing and making certain that the plants are well watered at the time they come into flower.

How are peony plants divided?

Dig the clumps carefully so as not to injure or bruise the roots. Wash off all the soil. With a heavy, sharp knife, cut each clump through the crown into several pieces. Each division should have several plump buds, which in the fall are approximately one-half inch long. Roots without such buds rarely produce plants.

Will peonies bloom the first summer after being transplanted?

Usually, if the plants are vigorous and were not divided into small pieces, but dividing is a severe operation, resulting in the loss of roots in which food is stored. Dividing at an improper time causes recovery to be especially slow. If the divisions are very small, it may take two to three years before the plants are vigorous enough to bloom, and the blooms may not be as large and perfect as those produced in succeeding years.

Why do peonies that are several years old fail to bloom?

The following conditions may prevent blooming: too deep planting; too much shade; poor drainage; need of dividing; root disease; botrytis blight disease; roots infested with nematodes; lack of fertilizer; lack of moisture; lack of sunlight; injury to buds due to late frosts.

How can you bring an old peony border back into bloom?

If the plants are very old, it is advisable to divide the clumps and replant them in well-prepared soil. Keep the bed free of weeds by maintaining a mulch and apply fertilizer in the spring to increase the quality and quantity of the flowers.

Should I disbud my peonies?

A peony stem usually has from three to seven buds. The main, or terminal, bud produces the largest and most perfect flower. If you wish this main bud to be particularly spectacular, pick off all other buds on that stem. Disbud when the plants are about eighteen inches tall, just as soon as the secondary buds become visible.

Do peonies need to be cultivated?

Very little cultivation is necessary, except to remove weeds. The best time to destroy weeds is very early in the spring before the plants have made much growth, or late in the fall after the tops have been cut off. A constant mulch will suppress most weeds.

Do peonies require much moisture?

A moderately moist soil is suitable. In the spring when the flowers are developing, if the natural rainfall is not abundant, thorough watering increases the size and quality of the flowers. It also tends to hasten flowering.

Is there any way to make the stems of peonies stronger?

Some otherwise fine varieties naturally have weak stems. There is little that can be done except to give them artificial support. It is also well to plant them in full sunlight (at least six hours a day), if possible, where they are protected from strong winds. They will also withstand light shade. Single-flowered varieties are more erect. Use special, circular wire plant supports, or tie individual stakes to each stem. Shake the water out of the peony heads after each rain. Planting in a location sheltered from the wind helps to prevent damage.

When should peony flowers be cut for use indoors?

Preferably in the early morning. For cutting, select buds that have just started to open. Do not take more stem than is actually required for the arrangement. It is advisable to leave at least two or three leaves below the point where the stem is cut.

Should the old flowers and seed pods of peonies be removed?

Yes, for two reasons. First, during the flowering season, old blossoms should be picked off before the petals fall, as this helps to control the botrytis blight disease. Second, seed pods compete with the roots for the food produced in the leaves.

The peony, with its variety of flower forms, attractive colors, clean habit of growth, and deep-green foliage, is an excellent choice for most gardens.

Maggie Oster

Should the foliage on peonies be cut back after the blooming season?

No. The foliage should not be cut until it has been killed by hard frosts. The food manufactured in the foliage is stored in the roots and thus helps produce flowers the following year. If the foliage is cut back shortly after blooming, the plants are deprived of their next year's food supply. An added advantage of leaving the foliage on is that the autumn coloring of peony leaves is usually quite attractive. Removing the *dead* leaves, however, helps to prevent the spread of disease, so it's an important task.

Should peonies be protected in the winter?

Peonies should be mulched the first year after planting so that they don't heave out of the ground. After plants are well established, no protection is necessary.

Are peonies hardy in cold climates?

They are among the hardiest of garden flowers, surviving winter minimum temperatures of -50° F.

What can I do to control ants that are eating the flower buds of my peonies?

Ants do not eat peony buds; they feed on the sweet, syrupy material secreted by the developing buds. They usually do not harm peonies although it's possible that they may spread botrytis blight disease.

Why do peony buds dry up without developing into blossoms? The plant seems disease free—the leaves are not dry and there is no sign of bud rot.

The problem is most likely botrytis blight, which can be prevented by carefully cleaning the peony bed in the fall and keeping it clean of dead leaves during all seasons. To control botrytis blight, spray the peonies with benomyl every fourteen days from the time the leaves show until the flowers open. Late frost in the spring can also kill buds, but disease is the more likely culprit.

Why do peony stalks wilt and fall over?

This is another symptom of botrytis blight. In wet weather, young shoots are often infected and become covered with gray mold, turn black, and rot at the base.

Why do peonies have brown spots on the petals?

This, too, is usually because of botrytis blight. Rain splashes spores from infected buds onto the opening blossoms, and everywhere a spore starts to germinate there is a brown spot on the petals. However, browning may also be due to thrips injury.

Why does foliage turn black after the blooming period?

It may, in a wet season, be due to botrytis blight. Blackening may also be due to stem rot, another fungus disease. Remove and destroy the infected shoots very carefully so as not to drop out any of the sclerotia, which are formed loosely in the pith (stem tissue) and fall out of the stalks.

What would cause roots to rot?

Possibly botrytis blight or stem rot, or sometimes a downy mildew that causes a wet rot of the crown. There is no chemical control. Peonies should not be planted in too wet soil; if you have heavy clay, lighten it with peat moss or other organic material. Never leave manure on as a mulch that shoots have to push up through.

How can I control rose chafers, the insects that have become troublesome around my peonies?

There is no very satisfactory answer to this universal question. Pick off as many as you can and spray your plants with Sevin or rotenone, repeating weekly as necessary. If it is any comfort to you, when the Japanese beetles get worse, the rose chafers diminish. (The same insecticides will somewhat control the beetles.)

Perennial cornflower: Shown here in front of pink Oriental poppies and lupine, blue cornflowers spread rapidly but not aggressively.

Perennial cornflower, Knapweed, Mountain bluet, Perennial bachelor's-button *(Centaurea)*

I'm developing a low-maintenance garden. Should I include the perennial cornflowers?

By all means. They tolerate a wide range of soils and full sun. Propagate by division.

Perennial forget-me-not *(Myosotis)*

Is there a perennial forget-me-not that will bloom all summer?

Myosotis scorpioides will bloom most of summer if located in shade beside a stream or pool. Plants grow about twelve inches tall, with both pink and blue flowers, and are hardy to -40° F. Divide in early spring, or sow seed directly where they will grow permanently.

Perennial sunflower *(Helianthus)*

Sunflowers are such cheerful plants, but the annual ones are too large for my garden. Is there something similar, but smaller, among perennial flowers?

Two types can be recommended for the home garden: the swamp sunflower *(H. angustifolius)* and *H. x multiflorus* varieties.

Cindy McFarland

What growing conditions do perennial sunflowers need?

Rich, deep, moist soil, and full sun to light shade. Fertilize each spring and divide every year.

Can you suggest some ways to use perennial sunflowers in the garden?

They are splendid at the back of the flower border, in clumps among shrubs, or naturalized along paths. They combine well with hardy asters and make good cut flowers.

Perennial sweet pea *(Lathyrus)*

Is it possible to grow perennial sweet pea from seed?

It is best started from seeds sown in autumn, preferably where they are to grow permanently, for the plant has long, fleshy roots and resents disturbance. Once established, it can be invasive, but by choosing a site carefully, you can readily enjoy its ten-foot, vinelike, gray-green foliage, and pink, rose, and white flowers. Try growing it on a lattice fence, as long as the slats are not too large for the tendrils to grasp. Special soil preparation or care is rarely needed. Hardy to -30° F., it requires only a sunny location and average garden soil.

I have a well-established perennial sweet pea that failed to bloom last year. How can I get it to produce blooms?

Try mixing superphosphate with the soil, six ounces per square yard.

Should hardy sweet peas be cut back in the fall?

They can be cut back to just above the ground level any time after the tops have dried up.

Phlox *(Phlox)*

Can you offer some tips on raising garden phlox?

Phlox grow best in a well-drained, humus-rich soil. They also need a fair amount of water. Cut off old flowers after they bloom. Lift, divide, and replant them about every three years, even more often for varieties that grow and spread rapidly. Phlox are subject to mildew; spray or dust regularly with an all-purpose insecticide-fungicide.

What are some of the ways to use the creeping phlox, moss pink? Do you have any tips for it?

The semievergreen, mat-forming moss pink *(P. subulata)* is covered with small flowers in April and May. It is hardy to -40° F. or lower. Because it grows only four to six inches tall, it is

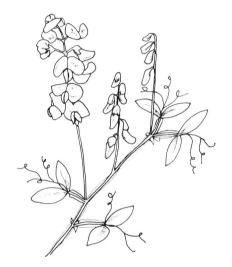

Perennial sweet pea: The hardy, ten-foot vines of perennial sweet pea will readily cover a lattice fence in a sunny garden with average soil.

excellent for use on slopes or banks, along the tops of rock walls, in rock gardens, or as an edging. It tolerates hot, dry conditions, but it should have as good a soil as possible and full sun. Trim plants after blooming is finished. The bright pink type is common, but there are many varieties in other shades of pink, red, white, and blue.

What is the best exposure for phlox?

Although they will grow in partial shade, a minimum of three or four hours of sun is desirable, and they thrive in full sun.

When is the best time to plant phlox?

Either in early fall or early spring. Container-grown phlox can be planted in midsummer. If planted in the fall, phlox should be mulched with a three-inch layer of leaves or straw, to prevent possible heaving from the ground as a result of freezing and thawing.

How should soil be prepared for phlox?

The soil should be dug to a depth of twelve to eighteen inches and mixed with a three-inch layer of rotted manure, leaf mold, or a mixture of peat moss and compost.

How far apart should phlox be planted?

Set the tall-growing varieties fifteen to eighteen inches apart, and allow three or four shoots to grow from each plant. Shorter-growing types should be planted twelve to fifteen inches apart.

Do phlox require extra water and fertilizer?

If the bed was well prepared by deep digging and the incorporation of organic matter, extra watering may not be necessary. They do respond to sidedressings of fertilizer or to applications of liquid fertilizers when the flower buds are about to form.

How can I handle garden phlox to get perfectly shaped, rather than ill-shaped, heads of blossoms?

Probably your plants are old and need lifting, dividing, and replanting. Thin out the shoots that appear in the spring, leaving several inches between those that are left. Give liquid fertilizer weekly. It is also possible that your phlox are a poor variety, or they could be infested with mites or nematodes.

In transplanting phlox, how deeply should they be set?

Because phlox roots should be planted straight down, dig the holes deep and give them plenty of space, but the crown should be no more than one or two inches below soil level.

Maggie Oster

Moss pink: This creeping phlox is covered with small flowers in April and May and makes an excellent rock garden plant.

Maggie Oster

Phlox: Cut off the faded flowers of phlox after bloom.

How can I propagate perennial phlox?

Propagate phlox by lifting plants from the soil and dividing them in the fall. Choose the new divisions from the outer edge of the clump and discard the old center, which is too woody for good growth. Replant them as you would new plants.

Why did my phlox change color? Many plants that were white, salmon, or deep red are now a sickly magenta.

You probably allowed the seeds to ripen and self-sow. Unfortunately, self-seeded phlox tend to revert to their ancestral purplish color. As these natural forms are usually exceptionally vigorous, they crowd out the desirable but less sturdy varieties. Cut off faded flowers to prevent reseeding, and weed out any seedlings that do appear.

Why don't my phlox thrive? The foliage is sometimes whitish looking, then it turns to brown. The lower leaves drop off and the blooms are poor.

Garden phlox are subject to red spider mite infestations, which cause a whitish appearance at first, then the leaves turn brown. They are also subject to mildew and a disease that causes the lower leaves to drop. Deep, rich, moist but well-drained soil, and periodic dusting with sulfur or spraying with Karathane, will help.

What is the cause of every bit of phlox foliage drying up, from roots to flower?

This question is almost universal, and there is no real answer. Rather than being caused by a specific organism, it is evidently a physiological disease, possibly due to a blockage of food and water movement at the point of union of new and old growth. To prevent, cut old stalks back to ground level in the fall or early spring.

A small, soft-bodied insect, orange with black stripes, attacks my phlox. Nothing seems to control it, and I have never been able to find out what it is. Do you know?

This is probably the phlox bug, a sucking insect with reddish or orange margins on the wings and a black stripe on the back. Kill the nymphs by spraying with malathion, Sevin, or insecticidal soap.

Pincushion flower (*Scabiosa*)

How tall does pincushion flower grow and what color are the flowers?

Pincushion flower grows eighteen to thirty inches tall. The richly textured, three-inch flowers borne on long stems in midsummer are usually pale blue, but there is also a white form, as well as darker blue and violet hybrids. Plants are hardy to -40° F.

What can I do to get more flowers on my pincushion flower?

Plant them in a light soil. Temperatures above 80° F. inhibit flowering, so give them light shade in hot regions; elsewhere full sun is preferable. Remove faded flowers.

When and how do I divide my pincushion flower?

Plants two or three years old can be divided by cutting or pulling the plants apart in early spring and replanting them.

Pincushion flower: These unusual flowers need to be shaded in regions with hot summers.

Plantain lily, Funkia (Hosta)

How can Hostas be used in my landscape?

For partial to fully shaded conditions no plant can compete with the hostas. They are grown mainly for their foliage, which comes in various shades of green, edged or patterned with white or yellow, and strongly textured. Many varieties have lovely flowers, resembling small lilies, in shades of white, lavender, or purple; some are fragrant. They range in height from six inches to over three feet. They are easy to propagate by division. Use them as edging plants, as ground covers, as striking accents, grouped under trees and shrubs, in rock gardens, along streams or woodland paths—or even in the flower border.

How should I prepare the ground before planting Hosta?

Work the soil to a depth of twelve inches, incorporating plenty of organic matter such as compost, leaf mold, or peat moss. The soil should be moist but well drained.

How hardy are Hostas?

Most are hardy to -40° F., although not all new varieties are proven under these conditions. A late frost may nip the leaves of *Hosta*; plants should be covered if frost is imminent.

Plume poppy (Macleaya)

A friend of mine once grew plume poppy and it spread rapidly. Is there something similar that isn't so invasive?

Although *M. microcarpa* is excellent for naturalizing, the much more "sedate" *M. cordata* is recommended more frequently for garden use. Hardy to -40° F. and growing six to eight feet tall, it is a bold, dramatic plant. Although it produces plumes of white flowers in midsummer, the plant is mainly grown for the leaves, which are large, lobed, and blue-green with silvery undersides.

What are the growing conditions necessary for plume poppy and how should I use it in my landscape?

Plume poppies grow best in a moist but well-drained soil with full sun, except in very hot climates, where light shade is preferred. Propagate from seed or by division. Although it can be used in the back of the border, its striking effect is perhaps most appreciated when given a spot as a specimen plant.

Prickly pear, Cholla *(Opuntia)*

Cacti are some of my favorite houseplants. Are there any kinds that are hardy outdoors other than in the Southwest?

Prickly pear, the hardiest, will withstand temperatures to -10° F. It has flat pads that grow about six inches tall. In early summer, it produces bright yellow, two-inch flowers; these are followed by red-purple fruits that last several months. Prickly pears must have very well-drained, sandy soil to survive wet winters. Use them in a rock garden, seashore garden, or the front of a flower border composed of other drought-tolerant plants, such as butterfly weed and gaillardia. To propagate, break off a whole pad and stick several inches of it into the soil.

Prickly pear: This drought-tolerant plant flourishes in sandy soils and seashore gardens.

Maggie Oster

Primrose *(Primula)*

How is the primrose used in the garden?

Mass them for greatest effect from their brilliant colored flowers, of many varieties, in spring and sometimes in fall.

What kind of soil do primroses need?

A fairly moist, humus-rich soil with added leaf mold or peat moss mixed with rich compost. Primroses should be planted in partial shade.

Do primroses need fertilizer?

Yes, they need a fairly fertile soil. Use well-rotted or dehydrated animal manure, or an organic fertilizer recommended for camellias and rhododendrons.

What summer care and winter protection do primroses need?

They should be given shade and not allowed to dry out in the summer. Most primroses are hardy to -20° F.

What time of year is best for dividing primroses?

In late spring after they have finished flowering, or in late summer when they have started to go dormant.

Purple coneflower *(Echinacea)*

What is the plant with rosy purple flowers that resembles gloriosa daisy?

Purple coneflower, a native to our prairies and open woodlands, adapts well to our gardens. Hardy to -40° F., the stiff three- to four-foot plants bear their daisylike flowers with downward-bending petals from July until frost. Provide full sun and average garden soil. Propagate by division.

Purple loosestrife *(Lythrum)*

Purple loosestrife is such a charming wildflower growing in wet meadows and along streams and ponds. Does it adapt to the garden very well?

Native to Europe, purple loosestrife has made itself at home in North America in places like you describe. Growing four to six feet tall and hardy to -40° F., it can be used in naturalized plantings with moist soil, and full sun to light shade, without becoming a pest. Even better, however, is to choose from cultivars, which are shorter-growing plants and tolerant of a wider range of growing conditions. Plants bloom for a long period in midsummer. Propagate these cultivated varieties by dividing in spring or fall.

Purple rockcress (*Aubrieta*)

Isn't there a purple-flowered, ground-hugging plant that blooms in early spring?

You're probably thinking of purple rockcress. It grows four to six inches tall and is covered with tiny leaves and brilliant purple, lavender, or rose flowers, depending on the variety.

How can purple rockcress be used in the garden?

Plant it as an edging to a perennial border, in the rock garden, at the top of a stone wall, or between stones of a path.

What are the growing requirements of purple rockcress?

Hardy to -30° F., it must have a sandy, well-drained soil, in sun or light shade. Transplant in fall or early spring. Immediately after plants flower, trim them back severely. Divide the plants in the fall or propagate from seed.

Queen-of-the-Prairie. See Meadowsweet.

Rock cress: An excellent rock garden plant, rock cress is also quite pleasantly fragrant.

Ann Reilly

Ragwort (*Ligularia*)

Where should I plant ragwort in my garden?

Ragwort must have very moist, humus-rich soil with light shade and plenty of space. Place plants two to three feet apart. Plant in the back of the flower border or at the edge of a pond or stream. They combine well with *Hostas*, Japanese iris, and royal fern. Propagate by division.

Red valerian. See Jupiter's-beard.

Rock cress (*Arabis*)

What is the creeping, white-flowered plant that blooms in the spring at the same time as basket-of-gold and purple rockcress?

This is rock cress. The variety of rock cress called Flore Pleno, a rock cress that grows six inches tall with dense gray foliage, bears fragrant flowers from early to late spring that are excellent for cutting. It is hardy to -40° F. Like other woolly-leaved plants, rock cress tends to rot in hot, humid climates.

How can I successfully grow rock cress?

Use rock cress along a rock wall or as an edging. Provide loose, well-drained soil. To encourage branching, cut plants back after flowering. Propagate by dividing the plants or by rooting cuttings in late spring.

Rose mallow *(Hibiscus)*

What is the plant with dinner-plate-size flowers?

The plant most likely to fit that description is rose mallow. The many hybrids of this plant are hardy to -20° F., grow three to eight feet tall, and have large gray-green leaves. The tropical-like flowers, which resemble a single hollyhock bloom, may measure from six to twelve inches across, and bloom from July to September. The colors range from white to shades of pink and red; often the flowers have an ''eye'' of a different color.

Where should I plant rose mallows?

They are easy to grow in moist, well-drained soil in full sun, although once established, they tolerate dry soil. Group them in masses, use them as specimen plants, or plant them among shrubs or at the back of large flower borders. Plant them at least two feet apart. In areas with winter minimum temperatures of 0 to -20° F., lightly mulch them before winter.

Rose mallow: These dramatic plants bloom from July through September.

How shall I treat rose mallow before and after flowering?

In the spring, dig in rotted leaf mold and bonemeal or superphosphate. After bloom, cut off faded flowers; prune plants back to the ground in the fall after frost.

How are rose mallows propagated?

Propagate by division, or sow seeds, two in a pot, and then plant established seedlings in the garden. They will take about three years to bloom.

Russian sage *(Perovskia)*

Russian sage's silver-gray foliage and spikes of tiny violet-blue flowers have such a delicate, airy effect in the flower border. What kind of soil and care does it need?

This perennial deserves to be much more widely planted. The three- to five-foot plants make a great addition to the back of the border. Semiwoody plants are hardy to -20° F. and need only sun and any well-drained soil.

Saxifrage *(Bergenia)*

On a trip to the south of France last spring I saw a low-growing plant with large, shiny, round leaves and spikes of pink flowers. Is it possible to grow it in the United States?

This is saxifrage, hardy to -50° F. Use it around shrubs or in the flower border. In many climates, the leaves of the twelve- to eighteen-inch-tall plants are evergreen.

Sea holly: Teasel-like sea holly is excellent for both fresh and dried arrangements.

I've not had much success growing saxifrage. What does it need to grow well?

Although it tolerates almost any soil, it does best in humus-rich, moist, well-drained soil with either full sun or light shade. To propagate, divide the clumps, cutting the thick stems apart with a sharp knife. Unfortunately, slugs favor the lush foliage.

Sea holly *(Eryngium)*

The photos of sea holly in catalogs look so interesting. Is it difficult to grow?

Sea holly's unusual flowers, with a prickly ruff surrounding a teasel-like center, make it an unusual addition to the garden as well as to fresh and dried bouquets. The plant's blue-gray color is also an asset in the garden.

It is actually quite easy to grow. Provide full sun, and sandy, only moderately fertile loam. Most species are hardy to -20° F. Plants may be started from seed or purchased; they do not divide readily and should not be moved once they are planted.

Sea lavender *(Limonium)*

How long will sea lavender stay in bloom?

Sea lavender bears twelve-inch-wide, eighteen-inch-tall sprays of tiny lilac flowers for eight weeks during summer. Use them fresh or dried in arrangements.

Is sea lavender difficult to grow?

No, it is very easy. Plants need only full sun and well-drained soil. Hardy to -40° F., the six- to nine-inch, low-growing, evergreen leaves form a rosette that is attractive in the front of the border or in the rock garden.

Can I start sea lavender from seed?

Yes, but it may be three years before plants flower. In the garden, plants sometimes self-sow. Once established, plants do not readily survive transplanting.

Sea pink. See Thrift.

Self-heal *(Prunella)*

Isn't self-heal a weed?

Most species can be pests, but *P. Webbiana* is a low-growing, nine- to twelve-inch plant that is useful in the shade garden or as a ground cover under trees and shrubs. It is easily grown, but does not readily get out of control. Plants bloom in midsummer with short, thick spikes of hooded flowers in shades of rose-purple, pink, lilac, and white. Plant in moist, humus-rich garden soil and propagate by division or from seeds.

Siberian bugloss *(Brunnera)*

Please describe Siberian bugloss.

Siberian bugloss is a lovely plant with blue flowers that complements daffodils and forsythias in the spring. Plants grow twelve to eighteen inches tall and are hardy to -40° F.

What are the best growing conditions for Siberian bugloss?

Let it naturalize among shrubs or trees. Plants tolerate dry to moist shade. Enrich the soil with organic matter, such as peat moss or compost.

Snake grass, Spiderwort, Widow's-tears *(Tradescantia)*

What growing conditions does snake grass require?

Plants are easily grown in humus-rich, moist but well-drained soil in light shade. They are hardy to -30° F. Propagate by division in spring or fall.

How big does snake grass get and when does it flower?

Most varieties grow eighteen to twenty-four inches tall. Plants bear three-petaled, one-inch flowers in early summer. If plants are cut back to the ground in midsummer, they will flower again in the fall. Flowers open in the morning and close by the afternoon.

Snakeroot. See Bugbane.

Sneezeweed *(Helenium)*

The bright yellow, daisylike flowers of sneezeweed, produced from summer into fall, are great in the garden, but the plants get so tall. Can I do anything about that?

Pinch out the growing tips in the spring to keep sneezeweed under three feet tall.

Where is the best place in the garden for sneezeweed?

It thrives in any soil in full sun. Consider using it in masses alone, or at the back of a large border or among shrubs. Excellent as cut flowers, sneezeweed also makes a good garden companion to Silver King artemisia, mist flower, butterfly bush, and rudbeckia. It is hardy to -40° F.

Maggie Oster

Snakegrass: Cut snakegrass back after the first midsummer bloom, and plants will flower again in fall.

What about the black bugs on sneezeweed?

Insects on sneezeweed are most often small black snout beetles, which start chewing the young shoots in early spring and often keep working until flowering. Spraying with a mixture of Sevin and Kelthane keeps them fairly well in check.

Snow-in-summer *(Cerastium)*

I need a low-growing plant as an edging. It must be able to survive dry, sunny conditions. What do you recommend?

Snow-in-summer is a popular plant for the conditions you describe. Growing about six inches high, it has white flowers and small, woolly, silver-colored leaves. Hardy to -30° F., it spreads rapidly. Plants are propagated by plant divisions made very early in the spring.

Snow-on-the-mountain, Gout weed, Bishop's weed *(Aegopodium)*

I need a vigorous ground cover that will succeed where nothing else seems to, in a narrow strip between the house and a concrete sidewalk. The plant does not have to be evergreen.

Snow-on-the-mountain will serve your needs very well. Hardy to -40° F., it grows twelve inches tall with white-edged green, three-parted leaves. You should be forewarned, however, that this plant spreads rapidly and aggressively and can become a real garden weed in some areas, particularly in the Northeast. Propagate by division.

Soapweed. See Yucca.

Solomon's-seal *(Polygonatum)*

What kind of soil and light does Solomon's-seal need?

Deep, moist but well-drained, humus-rich soil, and light shade. They survive minimum winter temperatures of -30° F. Propagate by division in early spring or fall. Solomon's-seal is a splendid plant to combine with rhododendrons and azaleas or with ferns, *Hostas*, and primroses.

Spanish bayonet. See Yucca.

Speedwell *(Veronica)*

There are so many different *Veronicas*. Can you sort them out for me?

This is a large group including both annuals and perennials. The perennial types all need moist but well-drained soil and full sun. They vary in height from ground hugging to two feet, but

Speedwell: This old-favorite perennial needs moist soil and full sun.

Maggie Oster

all are hardy to -40° F. and produce spiky flowers in shades of blue, pink, red, purple, and white. Two types are best for flower borders: Rosette-forming varieties, which form mats of toothed leaves with six- to eighteen-inch spikes of flowers in midsummer; and tall varieties, which grow to over fifteen inches in height, form vase-shaped clumps and flower in midsummer.

The crowns of my speedwells are rising above the surface of the ground. Can I remedy this?

Veronicas often do raise their crowns if left in the same spot for some time. Lift and replant them every two or three years.

My speedwells tend to sprawl. What can I do?

Some varieties do this more than others. To provide support, use commercially made round wire enclosures, or stick twigs in the soil around the plants when they are young.

How is speedwell propagated?

By division in the spring.

Spiderwort. See Snake grass.

Spotted dead nettle *(Lamium)*

Will spotted dead nettle become a terrible weed like some of its relatives?

L. maculatum seldom becomes a pest, but it is an excellent ground cover. It does best in partial shade, in any soil, and it tolerates drought well. Hardy to -40° F., plants grow about twelve inches tall. Flowers may be pink or white and resemble snapdragons, but spotted dead nettle is grown mainly for its foliage, which may be spotted with white or have other variegation. Divide plants in the spring.

Spurge *(Euphorbia)*

Someone told me that there are garden plants related to the Christmas poinsettia. What are they like?

Many *Euphorbias* do well in temperate perennial flower gardens. In climates with cool summers, cushion spurge forms a neat twelve- to eighteen-inch mound with chartreuse-yellow flowers in spring; it is hardy to -30° F. In climates with mild winters (minimum temperatures of 10° F.), *E. Characias Wulfenii* is a striking plant with its shrubby, evergreen, four-foot stems of tightly packed, blue-green leaves topped with chartreuse-yellow flowers.

What kind of soil does spurge need?

It does best in sandy, somewhat dry soils.

Spurge: The leaves of **Euphorbia Characias Wulfenii** *are evergreen.*

Maggie Oster

I've heard that spurge is poisonous. How toxic is it?

Euphorbia stems contain a milky sap that can cause skin irritation. Keep them away from the eyes, mouth, any cuts, and children.

Stokes' aster *(Stokesia)*

I'm fond of the lovely blue, two- to five-inch flowers of Stokes' aster for bouquets. Are the plants very hard to grow?

Stokes' aster is hardy to -20° F., but it must have well-drained soil to survive these winter temperatures. Otherwise, it is a relatively easy-to-grow plant. Provide sandy or light loam and full sun.

How long is the blooming period for Stokes' aster?

It depends on your location. In northern climates, it will bloom much of the summer; in the Southeast, during June; on the Gulf, through the winter; and in California, off and on all

Stokes' aster: In sandy soil and full sun, Stokes' aster will bloom off and on all summer in cool climates.

Maggie Oster

winter. Whatever the climate, faded flowers should be removed to extend the blooming period.

Are Stokes' aster blossoms ever any color other than blue?

Yes, there are white and purple forms, as well as less readily available pink and yellow forms. Plants grow twelve to twenty-four inches tall, with the most height coming in warmer climates.

How is Stokes' aster propagated?

Plants are easily raised from seed, but cultivars should be propagated by division.

Stonecrop *(Sedum)*

I've seen so many different looking plants labeled *Sedum*. What are the main ones to consider for my perennial garden?

Sedums are a large group of plants with fleshy, succulent leaves. They come in many different heights and flower colors, with various growth habits and hardiness tolerances. In general, *Sedums* are very easy to grow, thriving in full sun, and poor, dry soil. Most are hardy to -40° F. Autumn Joy is particularly popular. It has thick, bright green leaves on eighteen- to twenty-four-inch stems. In late summer, the large flower heads of pale pink gradually deepen to a rose-red. It is a favorite of bees and butterflies. The dried flower heads can be left on the plants for winter interest in the garden or cut for arrangements.

How should I use stonecrop in the landscape?

The low-growing forms are best used as an edging in the front of a flower border, cascading over stone walls, or planted in the rock garden. The taller kinds can be planted in masses alone or combined with other perennials.

How is stonecrop propagated?

From cuttings, divisions, layering, or seed.

Sundrops, Evening primrose *(Oenothera)*

Are sundrops, with their rich yellow flowers that bloom over so much of the summer, hard to grow?

About eighteen inches tall and hardy to -30° F., sundrops are easy to grow in any soil and full sun. Although they spread rapidly, they are easy to remove. The Ozark sundrop *(O. missourensis)* is a trailing plant with four-inch yellow flowers and attractive seed pods; grow these in dry soil only. Plants are propagated by seed or division in early spring.

Maggie Oster

Sundrops: This sunny, easy-to-grow flower spreads rapidly.

Someone told me there is an Oenothera that has flowers that change from white to pink. What is this?

The evening primrose *(O. speciosa)* has three-inch, white-to-pink flowers in late summer. Hardy to -20° F., this biennial readily self-sows and spreads rapidly by root runners as well. Choose a sunny location where it can grow unrestrained.

Sunrose *(Helianthemum)*

I have heard about a small plant, ideal for edging the flower border, that is evergreen and has pink, yellow, or red flowers. What is it?

You're referring to the various kinds of sunrose. Growing about ten inches tall and hardy to -20° F., they need full sun, and a light, heavily limed soil. Where temperatures normally go as low as -20° F., plants should be mulched before the winter. They bear one-inch, pink, yellow, copper-red, or white flowers, which open in the morning, from midsummer to fall.

What care does sunrose need?

Heavily prune back plants immediately after flowering or in early spring. They do not transplant well. Propagate from cuttings taken in spring or summer.

Sweet rocket. See Dame's-rocket.

Sweet william. See Carnations.

Sweet woodruff *(Asperula)*

I've had trouble getting anything to grow under some pine trees. Would sweet woodruff grow there?

Yes. It will quickly spread as a ground cover in shade with moist, humus-rich, acid soil. Contain the roots if you don't want them to spread. The whorled leaves of sweet woodruff grow six to twelve inches tall and are hardy to -40° F. Propagate by division.

Thrift, Sea pink *(Armeria)*

On a recent visit to Seattle, I saw plants that resembled chives. What might they have been?

The evergreen tufts of grasslike leaves with globe-shaped, early summer flowers in shades of pink, rose, and white are called thrift, or sea pink.

Will sea pinks grow near the seashore only?

No, but they do need very well-drained, sandy soil in full sun. The species may be propagated by seed, but cultivars should be divided in order to be certain of getting the desired strain.

Thrift: Evergreen thrift prefers well-drained, sandy soil in full sun.

Tickseed *(Coreopsis)*

I have heard that tickseed is one of the best perennials. Is this really so? Are some varieties better than others?

Tickseed is an excellent plant, producing bright yellow, daisylike flowers off and on all summer long, if the faded flowers are removed. It is not particular as to soil, but needs full sun. The best species to grow is *C. verticillata*, the threadleaf coreopsis, which is hardy to -40° F. Plants grow twelve to thirty-six inches tall. All the tickseeds make excellent cut flowers. In the flower garden, a favorite combination is tickseed planted with Shasta daisies in front of delphiniums.

Can tickseed be started from seed?

Yes. If seeds are sown in early spring indoors, the plants will bloom the first year. You can also plant it outdoors in summer for bloom next year. Plants may be propagated by division.

Toadflax *(Linaria)*

Is there a perennial that looks like a yellow snapdragon?

This sounds like toadflax, the cultivated relative of the wild-flower known as butter-and-eggs. Blooming from early to mid-

Ann Reilly

Turtlehead: Keep these native plants short and bushy by pinching out their growing tips when the stems are about six inches tall.

summer with lemon-yellow flowers, it grows thirty inches tall and has blue-green leaves. Plants are hardy to -40° F.

How do I grow toadflax?

Provide full sun and any well-drained soil. Propagate plants from seed or by division in early spring. Plants will self-sow but seldom become a weed. Consider combining it with blue-flowering plants like sage, globe thistle, and flax.

Turtlehead (*Chelone*)

I am trying to grow as many native plants as possible in my flower border. A neighbor told me of a plant called turtlehead. Can you tell me more about it?

Turtlehead deserves to be more widely grown. Three feet tall with glossy, dark green leaves, it is hardy to -40° F. The pink flowers, in clusters at the top of the stems, do indeed resemble a turtle with its mouth open.

I planted turtlehead in a sunny border and it died. What did I do wrong?

Chelones thrive best in moist, humus-rich soil in partial shade. Extra fertilizer, water, and mulch should be applied at blooming time. To get shorter plants, pinch out the growing tips when stems are six inches tall. Propagate from seeds, cuttings, or division of the roots in spring.

Violet (*Viola*)

Are violets just small versions of the familiar pansy?

For all practical purposes, yes. In general, violets have smaller flowers than pansies and are hardier, surviving minimum winter temperatures of -30° F., with a few exceptions.

What are the basic growing requirements of violets?

Most grow best under cool conditions in humus-rich, moist but well-drained soil in light shade. They are often used in rock and wildflower gardens as well as at the front of flower borders. Hot, exposed locations are not conducive to good results. Work in plenty of peat moss or leaf mold before planting violets.

Why do the plants grow up out of the soil instead of staying in it?

The plants root at the surface, with the crown above. As they develop, the crown rises still higher above the soil.

What is the proper time to plant violet seed for spring bloom?

Outdoors, in the latter part of summer; protect seedlings with a heavy mulch. Indoors, start them in late winter.

How may large blooms and long stems be produced?

Long stems and good flowers are produced on young, well-developed plants in a rich but well-drained soil. Thin out old plants in the spring.

Virginia bluebells *(Mertensia)*

Drifts of bluebells are so lovely in the spring. How can I best use them in my garden design?

The nodding flowers of Virginia bluebells are wonderful naturalized in woodland areas interplanted with daffodils and rhododendrons. These plants also combine well with hostas, which will fill in and be attractive after the bluebells go dormant.

What are the growing requirements of Virginia bluebells?

Hardy to -40° F., bluebells grow one to two feet tall and bloom in early spring. They need moist, humus-rich, deep soil, and naturalize well under deciduous trees and shrubs. To propagate, sow seeds immediately after they ripen or divide plants during their summer dormancy, marking them in spring so you can find them. Where slugs are a pest, they will find the bluebells.

Widow's-tears. See Snake grass.

Wild ginger *(Asarum)*

Will wild ginger grow as a ground cover in shade?

That is its best use. Hardy to -20° F., these six-inch, ground-hugging plants with glossy, kidney-shaped leaves are attractive and durable. Soil should be moist and humus-rich. Plants spread by rhizomes, and plantings can be increased easily in the spring by division.

Windflower, Japanese anemone *(Anemone)*

Are there any good fall-blooming perennials besides chrysanthemums and asters?

There are several that are very good, including the windflower, or Japanese anemone. Two to four feet tall, with white, pink, or red flowers, windflower has dark green foliage.

What kind of growing conditions do Japanese anemones need?

Plant them in a humus-rich, moist but well-drained soil. They seem to thrive best when planted in front of evergreen or deciduous shrubs or walls facing south. They need sun, but will tolerate afternoon shade. Water them during dry weather. Although they are hardy to -20° F., a light covering of leaves is often beneficial. Propagate by dividing the roots or sowing seed in spring.

Windflower: This is an excellent fall-blooming plant, available in white, pink, or red.

Maggie Oster

How can one protect windflowers from the blister beetle?

Only by constant vigilance when the beetles appear in mid-summer. Dust or spray with Sevin or insecticidal soap. Pyrethrum-rotenone sprays are also helpful, as is handpicking of the beetles.

Wormwood, Mugwort *(Artemisia)*

I recently saw a lovely perennial border with flowers in shades of pink, yellow, blue, and lavender. What really set the colors off were several different types of gray-leaved plants. What might some of these have been?

Some of the best gray-leaved plants belong to the genus *Artemisia*. Some favorites are southernwood *(A. Abrotanum)* and wormwood *(A. Absinthium)*, both of which do best in full sun, in any well-drained soil. Propagate by division.

The local herb society sells wreaths made of Silver King artemisia. Is this hard to grow?

Silver King artemisia *(A. ludoviciana)* is very easy to grow. Hardy to -30° F., its branched stems grow about three feet tall with silver-gray leaves. Plant in full sun in any well-drained soil.

Yarrow: Excellent either as a fresh cut flower or for drying, yarrow is easy to grow and relatively pest free.

Maggie Oster

Yarrow (*Achillea*)

Can you recommend a plant with finely cut foliage and flowers that are excellent for cutting and drying?

Consider the many yarrows. These long-blooming plants are hardy to -40° F., grow two to five feet tall, tolerate dry soil, and do best in full sun. To dry them, cut the flower heads before the pollen forms.

Do yarrows need any special care?

Yarrows are relatively pest free, but the taller kinds may need a little support. This is easily provided by sticking a few twiggy branches into the soil around the plants in spring.

What is the best way to propagate yarrow?

The clumps of yarrow are easily divided, in either spring or fall. Plants may also be started from seeds, which, if sown early, will bloom the same year.

Yucca, Spanish bayonet, Adam's needle, Soapweed (*Yucca*)

How old (from seed) must a yucca plant be to blossom? Will it bloom frequently?

Yucca blooms when it is about four to five years old. After that the clump should bloom every year or at least every second year.

What kind of soil and light do yuccas need?

These stately perennials with evergreen, sword-shaped leaves and bold flower spikes of white bells need well-drained soil and full sun. They will tolerate very poor sandy soil and are almost indestructible once established. The clumps of leaves are usually two feet tall and the flower spike adds another two to four feet of height.

What is the preferred time for moving yuccas?

It is best done in early spring, when the plant is dormant, but even then it is not easy. Detach young suckers or divide old clumps.

I have several yucca plants that were on the property when we moved here five years ago. Why don't they bloom?

Perhaps they don't get enough sun or the soil is too heavy.

Maggie Oster

Yucca: Although yucca takes several years to bloom after being planted, it is almost indestructible once established.

Perennials Planting Guide

COMMON NAME	GENUS, SPECIES	ZONE	PLANT HEIGHT UNDER 2'	2-3'	OVER 3'	CUT FLOWERS
Astilbe	*Astilbe x Arendsii*	4		x		
Avens	*Geum* species	6	x			
Baby's-breath	*Gypsophila paniculata*	3		x		x
Balloon flower	*Platycodon grandiflorus*	3	x			x
Basket-of-gold	*Aurinia saxatilis*	3	x			
Bear's-breech	*Acanthus mollis*	8			x	
Beard-tongue						
Common	*Penstemon barbatus*	3	x	x		x
Bedding	*P. x gloxinioides*	7	x			x
Bee balm	*Monarda didyma*	4			x	x
Bellflower						
Carpathian bellflower	*Campanula carpatica*	3	x			
Dane's-blood	*C. glomerata*	3		x		x
Canterbury-bells	*C. Medium*	3		x		
Peachleaf bells	*C. persicifolia*	3	x	x		x
Scotch harebell	*C. rotundifolia*	2	x			
Betony	*Stachys grandiflora*	3	x			x
Lamb's ears	*S. byzantina*	4	x			
Bishop's hat	*Epimedium* species	4	x			
Blackberry lily	*Belamcanda chinensis*	5		x		
Blanket flower	*Gaillardia x grandiflora*	3	x	x		x
Bleeding-heart						
	Dicentra eximia	3	x			x
	D. formosa	3	x			x
	D. spectabilis	2		x		x
Blue plumbago	*Ceratostigma plumbaginoides*	5-6	x			
Blue stars	*Amsonia Tabernaemontana*	3		x		x
Bugbane						
Cohosh bugbane	*Cimicifuga racemosa*	3			x	x
Kamchatka bugbane	*C. simplex*	3			x	x
Bugleweed	*Ajuga reptans*	3	x			
Bugloss	*Anchusa azurea* var.	3	x	x	x	x
Butterfly flower	*Asclepias tuberosa*	3		x		x
Campion						
Maltese cross	*Lychnis chalcedonica*	3		x		x
Rose campion	*L. Coronaria*	3		x		
Catchfly	*L. Viscaria*	3	x			
Candytuft	*Iberis sempervirens*	3	x			
Carnation						
Allwood pinks	*Dianthus x Allwoodii*	4	x			x
Sweet william	*D. barbatus*	5	x			x
Maiden pinks	*D. deltoides*	4	x			x
Cottage pinks	*D. plumarius*	3	x			x
Carolina lupine	*Thermopsis caroliniana*	3			x	x
Catmint	*Nepeta x Faassenii*	3	x			
Chinese forget-me-not	*Cynoglossum nervosum*	5	x			
Chinese-lantern plant	*Physalis Franchetii*	3		x		x

(continued)

FLOWER COLOR	FLOWER SEASON			LIGHT			SOIL		
	SPRING	SUMMER	FALL	SUN	PARTIAL SHADE	SHADE	DRY	MOIST, WELL-DRAINED	WET
white, pink, red		x			x			x	
orange, yellow	x	x		x	x			x	
white		x		x				x	
white, blue, pink		x		x	x			x	
yellow	x			x			x	x	
white, lilac, rose		x		x				x	
red, pink, purple		x		x			x	x	
red		x		x			x	x	
red, pink, white		x		x	x			x	
white, blue		x	x	x	x			x	
violet		x		x	x			x	
blue, white, rose		x		x	x			x	
white, blue		x		x	x			x	
blue		x		x	x			x	
pink		x		x				x	
pink		x		x			x	x	
red, yellow, white	x				x			x	
orange		x		x				x	
red, yellow		x	x	x			x	x	
pink		x	x	x	x			x	
pink		x	x	x	x			x	
pink, white	x			x	x			x	
blue		x	x	x	x			x	
blue	x			x	x			x	x
white		x			x	x		x	
white			x		x	x		x	
white, blue		x			x			x	
blue		x	x	x	x			x	
orange		x		x				x	
red		x		x	x			x	
magenta		x		x				x	
white, red		x		x				x	
white	x	x		x				x	
salmon	x	x		x				x	
white, pink, red	x	x		x				x	
pink	x	x		x				x	
white, pink, red	x	x		x				x	
yellow		x		x			x	x	
lavender		x		x				x	
blue		x		x				x	
orange			x	x	x			x	

Perennials Planting Guide

COMMON NAME	GENUS, SPECIES	ZONE	PLANT HEIGHT UNDER 2'	2-3'	OVER 3'	CUT FLOWERS
Christmas rose						
Stinking hellebore	*Helleborus foetidus*	6	x			
Corsican rose	*H. lividus corsicus*	8	x			
Christmas rose	*H. niger*	3	x			
Lenten rose	*H. orientalis*	4	x			
Chrysanthemum	*Chrysanthemum x morifolium*	4-5	x	x	x	x
Painted daisy	*C. coccineum*	3		x		x
Shasta daisy	*C. x superbum*	4		x		x
Cinquefoil	*Potentilla* species	4	x			
Columbine	*Aquilegia* hybrids	4		x		x
Coneflower	*Rudbeckia* species	3		x		x
Coralbells	*Heuchera* varieties	3	x			x
Cranesbill						
Spotted	*Geranium maculatum*	4	x			
Bloodred	*G. sanguineum*	3	x			
Cupid's-dart	*Catananche caerulea*	4	x			x
Dame's-rocket	*Hesperis matronalis*	3			x	x
Daylily	*Hemerocallis* species	3	x	x	x	
Delphinium						
	Delphinium x Belladonna	3		x	x	x
	D. elatum	2		x	x	x
	D. grandiflorum	3		x		x
Desert-candle	*Eremurus* species	4&6			x	x
False dragonhead	*Physostegia virginiana*	4		x		x
False indigo	*Baptisia australis*	3			x	x
False starwort	*Boltonia asteroides*	3			x	x
Ferns						
Maidenhair	*Adiantum pedatum*	3	x			
Lady	*Athyrium Filix-femina*	3		x		
Japanese painted	*A. Goeringianum* Pictum	3	x			
Hay-scented	*Dennstaedtia punctilobula*	3		x		
Wood	*Dryopteris* species	3		x		
Ostrich	*Matteuccia pensylvanica*	3			x	
Sensitive	*Onoclea sensibilis*	3		x		
Cinnamon	*Osmunda cinnamomea*	3			x	
Royal	*O. regalis* var. *spectabilis*	3			x	
Common	*Polypodium virginianum*	3	x			
Christmas	*Polystichum acrostichoides*	3	x			
Flax						
Golden	*Linum flavum*	5	x			
Blue	*L. perenne*	5	x			
Fleabane	*Erigeron* hybrids	5-6		x		x
Foxglove						
Yellow	*Digitalis grandiflora*	3			x	x
Merton's	*D. x mertonensis*	5			x	x
Common	*D. purpurea*	5			x	x
Gas plant	*Dictamnus albus*	3		x		x
Gay-feather	*Liatris* species	3		x	x	x
Gentian	*Gentiana* species	3	x			
Globeflower	*Trollius* species	3		x		x

| FLOWER COLOR | FLOWER SEASON | | | LIGHT | | | SOIL | | |
	SPRING	SUMMER	FALL	SUN	PARTIAL SHADE	SHADE	DRY	MOIST, WELL-DRAINED	WET
	X				X	X		X	
	X				X	X		X	
	X				X	X		X	
	X				X	X		X	
all but blue			X	X				X	
white, pink, red	X	X		X				X	
white		X		X				X	
pink, yellow, red		X	X	X	X			X	
red, blue, yellow, white, pink	X	X		X	X			X	
yellow		X	X	X				X	
red, pink				X	X			X	
pink		X		X				X	
pink		X		X				X	
blue		X		X			X		
purple, white		X		X	X			X	
yellow, orange, red		X	X	X	X			X	
blue		X		X	X				
blue, purple, pink, white		X		X	X				
white, blue		X		X	X				
white, pink, yellow		X		X				X	
white, pink		X	X	X	X			X	
blue		X		X			X	X	
white			X	X				X	
					X	X		X	
				X	X			X	
					X	X		X	
					X	X		X	
					X	X		X	
					X	X		X	
				X	X			X	
					X	X		X	X
					X	X		X	X
					X	X		X	X
					X	X		X	
yellow		X		X				X	
blue		X		X				X	
blue, pink		X		X			X	X	
yellow		X			X			X	
pink		X			X			X	
purple, pink		X			X			X	
pink, white		X		X				X	
white, pink		X	X	X				X	
blue		X			X			X	
yellow				X	X			X	X

135

Perennials Planting Guide

COMMON NAME	GENUS, SPECIES	ZONE	PLANT HEIGHT UNDER 2'	2-3'	OVER 3'	CUT FLOWERS
Globe thistle	*Echinops Ritro*	3			X	X
Goatsbeard	*Aruncus sylvester*	3			X	
Golden marguerite	*Anthemis tinctoria*	3		X		X
Goldenrod	*Solidago* hybrids	4		X		X
Greek valerian	*Polemonium caeruleum*	3		X		
Hardy aster	*Aster* varieties	4-5		X	X	X
Hardy begonia	*Begonia grandis*	6	X			
Hardy fuchsia	*Fuchsia magellanica*	7			X	
Hardy orchid	*Bletilla*	3	X			X
Hen-and-chickens	*Sempervivum tectorum*	4	X			
Hollyhock	*Alcea rosea*	3			X	
Iris	*Iris* species	3-4	X	X	X	X
Jupiter's-beard	*Centranthus ruber*	4		X		X
Lady's-mantle	*Alchemilla mollis*	3	X			X
Lavender cotton	*Santolina Chamaecyparissus*	5	X			
Leopard's-bane	*Doronicum caucasicum*	3	X			X
Lily-of-the-valley	*Convallaria majalis*	2	X			X
Lily-turf	*Liriope Muscari*	6	X			
Lobelia						
Cardinal flower	*Lobelia Cardinalis*	3			X	
Great blue lobelia	*L. siphilitica*	4		X		
Loosestrife gooseneck	*Lysimachia clethroides*	3		X		
Yellow	*L. punctata*	5		X		
Lungwort	*Pulmonaria* species	4	X			
Lupine	*Lupinus polyphyllus*	4			X	X
Mallow						
Hollyhock mallow	*Malva Alcea* var. *fastigiata*	4			X	
Musk mallow	*M. moschata*	3			X	
Marsh marigold	*Caltha palustris*	3	X			
Meadow rue	*Thalictrum aquilegifolium*	5		X		X
Yunnan	*T. Delavayi*	4			X	X
Lavender mist	*T. Rochebrunianum*	5			X	X
Meadowsweet	*F. vulgaris* Flore	3	X			
Queen-of-the-prairie	*Filipendula rubra* Venusta	2			X	
Queen-of-the-meadow	*F. Ulmaria* Flore Pleno	3			X	
Mist flower	*Eupatorium coelestinum*	6	X			X
Joe-Pye weed	*E. purpureum*				X	
Monkshood						
Azure	*Aconitum Fisheri*	3		X		
Common	*A. Napellus*	3		X		X
Orange sunflower	*Heliopsis scabra*	4			X	
Oriental poppy	*Papaver orientale*	3		X	X	X
Ornamental grasses						
Giant reed	*Arundo Donax*	7			X	
Feather Reed	*Calamagrostis acutiflora* Stricta	5			X	X

FLOWER COLOR	FLOWER SEASON SPRING	SUMMER	FALL	SUN	LIGHT PARTIAL SHADE	SHADE	DRY	SOIL MOIST, WELL-DRAINED	WET
blue		X	X	X			X	X	
white		X			X				X
yellow		X		X	X		X		
yellow			X	X			X	X	
white, blue	X	X		X	X			X	
white, pink, purple, blue, red			X	X				X	
pink		X	X		X			X	
purple, red		X			X			X	
pink		X			X			X	
pink		X		X			X	X	
pink, red, yellow, white		X		X	X			X	
all colors	X	X		X	X			X	
white, red		X		X	X			X	
yellow-green		X			X		X	X	
yellow		X	X	X			X	X	
yellow	X			X	X			X	
pink, white	X				X	X		X	
lavender		X	X		X			X	
red		X	X	X	X			X	X
blue		X	X	X	X			X	
white		X		X	X			X	
yellow		X		X	X			X	
pink, white, blue, red	X				X	X		X	
blue, pink, red, white, yellow		X		X				X	
pink, white		X		X				X	
pink, white		X		X				X	
yellow	X				X	X			X
pink, white	X	X		X	X			X	
mauve		X	X	X	X			X	
mauve		X	X	X	X			X	
white		X		X	X				
white, pink		X		X	X			X	
white		X		X	X				
lavender			X	X	X			X	
purple			X		X	X			X
blue			X	X	X			X	
blue, white	X	X		X	X			X	
orange, yellow		X	X	X			X	X	
orange, red, pink, white		X		X				X	
red		X		X				X	
beige		X	X	X				X	

137

Perennials Planting Guide

COMMON NAME	GENUS, SPECIES	ZONE	PLANT HEIGHT UNDER 2'	2-3'	OVER 3'	CUT FLOWERS
Japanese sedge	*Carex Morrowii* var. *expallida*	5	x			
Pampas	*Cortaderia Selloana*	7			x	x
Ravenna	*Erianthus ravennae*	6			x	x
Blue fescue	*Festuca ovina* var. *glauca*	4	x			
Eulalia	*Miscanthus sinensis*	4			x	x
Variegated purple moor	*Molinia caerulea*	4		x		x
Fountain	*Pennisetum alopecuroides*	5			x	x
Giant feather	*Stipa gigantea*	5			x	x
Ribbon	*Phalaris arundinacea* var. *picta*	3	x			
Ornamental onion	*Allium senescens*	3	x			x
Chives	*A. Schoenoprasum*	4	x			x
Garlic chives	*A. tuberosum*	4	x			x
Pearly everlasting	*Anaphalis margaritacea*	3	x			x
Peony	*Paenoia* species	3		x		x
Perennial cornflower						
John Coutts	*Centaurea hypoleuca*	3		x		x
Knapweed	*C. macrocephala*	2-3			x	x
Mountain bluet	*C. montana*	2-3		x		x
Perennial forget-me-not	*Myosotis scorpioides*	3	x			
Perennial sunflower	*Helianthus x multiflorus*	4			x	x
Swamp sunflower	*H. angustifolius*	6			x	x
Perennial sweet pea	*Lathyrus latifolius*	4			x	x
Phlox						
Early	*Phlox carolina*	3		x		x
Wild blue	*P. divaricata*	3	x			x
Garden	*P. paniculata*	3		x	x	x
Creeping	*P. stolonifera*	3	x			
Moss pink	*P. subulata*	3	x			
Pincushion flower	*Scabiosa caucasica*	3		x		x
Plantain lily	*Hosta* species	3	x			
Plume poppy	*Macleaya cordata*	3			x	
Prickly pear	*Opuntia humifusa*	6	x			
Primrose	*Primula* species	5	x			
Purple coneflower	*Echinacea purpurea*	3			x	x
Purple loosestrife	*Lythrum Salicaria*	3			x	
Purple rockcress	*Aubrieta deltoidea*	4	x			
Ragwort	*Ligularia* species	4		x		
Rock cress	*Arabis procurrens*	4	x			
Double rock cress	*A. caucasica* Flore Pleno	3	x			x
Rose mallow	*Hibiscus Moscheutos*	5			x	
Rue	*Ruta graveolens*	4	x			
Russian sage	*Perovskia atriplicifolia*	5		x		x
Saxifrage	*Bergenia cordifolia*	2	x			
	B. crassifolia	2	x			
Sea holly	*Eryngium* hybrids	5		x		x
Sea lavender	*Limonium latifolium*	3	x			x
Self-heal	*Prunella Webbiana*	4	x			
Siberian bugloss	*Brunnera macrophylla*	3	x			

FLOWER COLOR	FLOWER SEASON			LIGHT			SOIL		
	SPRING	SUMMER	FALL	SUN	PARTIAL SHADE	SHADE	DRY	MOIST, WELL-DRAINED	WET
white		X		X				X	
white		X	X	X				X	
silver, purple		X		X				X	
white		X		X				X	
beige		X	X	X				X	
beige		X	X	X				X	
silver-rose		X	X	X				X	
yellow		X	X	X				X	
white		X	X	X				X	
mauve		X		X				X	
pink		X		X				X	
white		X		X				X	
white		X	X		X		X		
white, red, pink	X	X		X				X	
mauve		X		X			X	X	
yellow		X		X			X	X	
blue		X		X			X	X	
blue, pink		X			X				X
yellow			X	X	X			X	
yellow			X	X	X			X	
pink		X	X	X				X	
white, pink, red		X		X	X			X	
blue	X	X		X	X			X	
pink, red, white		X	X	X	X			X	
pink, white, red, blue	X	X			X			X	
pink, white, red, blue	X	X		X				X	
blue, white, purple		X	X	X				X	
lavender, white		X			X	X		X	
white		X		X	X			X	
yellow		X		X			X		
white, red, blue, pink, yellow	X				X	X		X	
pink		X	X	X				X	
purple		X		X	X			X	
red, purple	X			X	X			X	
yellow		X		X	X			X	
white	X			X			X	X	
white	X			X			X	X	
pink, white, red		X	X	X	X			X	
yellow		X		X				X	
violet-blue		X		X			X	X	
pink	X			X	X			X	
pink	X			X	X			X	X
gray-blue		X	X	X			X	X	
lavender		X	X	X			X	X	
pink, white		X				X		X	
blue	X				X	X	X	X	

139

Perennials Planting Guide

COMMON NAME	GENUS, SPECIES	ZONE	UNDER 2'	2-3'	OVER 3'	CUT FLOWERS
Snake grass	*Tradescantia x Andersoniana*	4	x			
Sneezeweed	*Helenium autumnale*	3			x	x
Snow-in-summer	*Cerastium tomentosum*	4	x			
Snow-on-the-Mountain	*Aegopodium Podagraria* Variegatum	3	x			
Solomon's-seal	*Polygonatum* species	4		x	x	
Speedwell	*Veronica* species	3	x			x
Spotted dead nettle	*Lamium maculatum*	3	x			
Spurge	*Euphorbia Characias* Wulfenii	8			x	
Baby's breath	*E. corollata*	3		x		
Cushion	*E. epithymoides*	4	x			
Stokes' aster	*Stokesia laevis*	5	x			x
Stonecrop						
Aizoon	*Sedum Aizoon*	5	x			
Autum Joy	*Sedum* species	3		x		x
Kamtschat	*S. kamtschaticum*	3	x			
Ruby Glow	*Sedum* species	3	x			
Siebold	*S. Sieboldii*	3	x			
Showy	*S. spectabile*	3		x		x
Creeping	*S. spurium*	3	x			
Sundrops						
Ozark	*Oenothera missourensis*	4	x			
Evening primrose	*O. speciosa*	5	x			
Common	*O. tetragona*	4	x			
Sunrose	*Helianthemum nummularium*	5	x			
Sweet woodruff	*Asperula odorata*	3	x			
Thrift	*Armeria pseudarmeria*	6	x			
Sea pink	*A. maritima*	3	x			
Tickseed	*Coreopsis grandiflora/lanceolata*	5	x	x	x	x
Threadleaf	*C. verticillata*	3	x	x	x	x
Toadflax	*Linaria genistifolia*	3		x		x
Turtlehead	*Chelone Lyonii*	3			x	
Violet	*Viola* species	4	x			x
Virginia bluebells	*Mertensia virginica*	3	x			
Wild ginger	*Asarum europaeum*	5	x			
Windflower						
Japanese anemone	*Anemone x hybrida* var.	5		x	x	x
Pasque flower	*A. Pulsatilla*	5	x			x
Japanese anemone	*A. vitifolia* Robustissima	4		x		x
Wormwood	*Artemisia Absinthium*	3		x		
Southernwood	*A. Abrotanum*	5			x	
Silver King	*A. Ludoviciana*	4		x		
Silver Mound	*A. Schmidtiana*	3	x			
Yarrow	*Achillea*					
Fernleaf	*A. filipendulina*	3		x		x
Rosy	*A. Millefolium*	2	x			x
Sneezewort	*A. Ptarmica*	3		x		x
Woolly	*A. tomentosa*	3	x			
Yucca	*Yucca* species	3,5			x	

(continued)

FLOWER COLOR	FLOWER SEASON			SUN	LIGHT PARTIAL SHADE	SHADE	DRY	SOIL MOIST, WELL-DRAINED	WET
	SPRING	SUMMER	FALL						
blue, white, pink, purple	x				x	x		x	
yellow, red			x	x				x	
white		x		x			x	x	
white		x			x			x	
white	x	x			x	x		x	
blue, pink, white, purple		x		x				x	
pink	x	x		x	x			x	
ycllow	x			x				x	
white		x		x				x	
yellow	x			x				x	
blue, white		x	x	x			x	x	
yellow	x	x		x			x	x	
red			x	x			x	x	
yellow		x	x	x			x	x	
red			x	x			x	x	
pink			x	x			x	x	
pink, red, white		x	x	x			x	x	
red, pink		x		x			x	x	
yellow		x		x				x	
pink		x						x	
yellow		x		x				x	
pink, yellow, red		x		x				x	
white	x				x	x		x	
pink, white	x	x		x			x		
pink, white, red	x			x			x		
yellow		x		x			x	x	
yellow		x		x			x	x	
yellow		x		x				x	
pink		x	x	x	x			x	x
white, purple, pink, yellow	x				x			x	
blue	x				x			x	
maroon	x					x		x	
white, pink			x		x			x	
lilac	x				x			x	
pink			x		x			x	
yellow		x		x			x	x	
yellow		x		x			x	x	
yellow		x		x			x	x	
yellow		x		x			x	x	
yellow		x		x			x	x	
white, rose	x	x		x			x	x	
white		x		x			x	x	
yellow	x	x		x				x	
white		x		x			x	x	

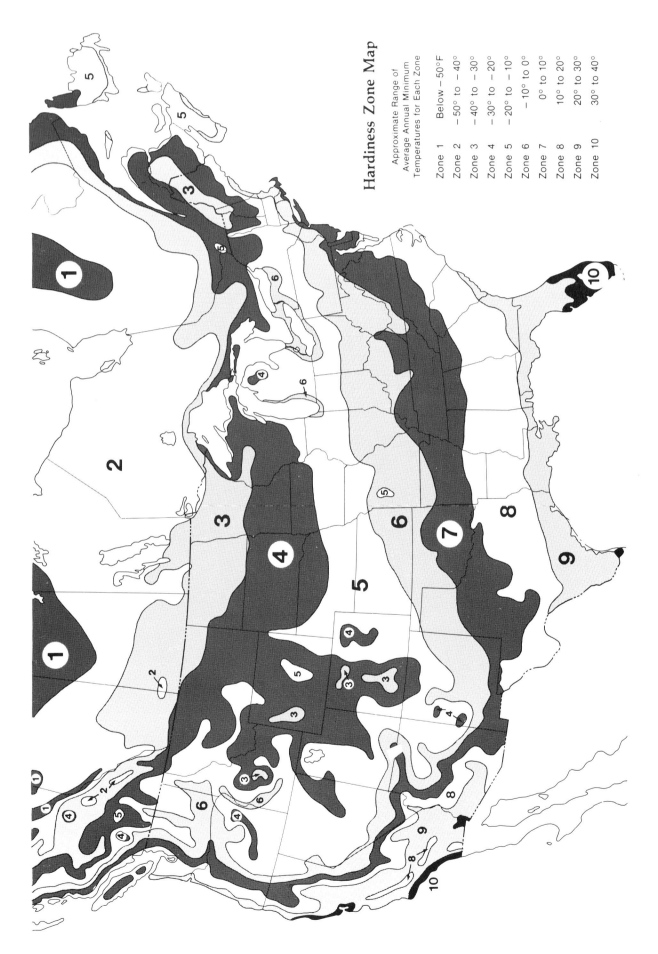

Hardiness Zone Map

Approximate Range of
Average Annual Minimum
Temperatures for Each Zone

Zone 1   Below −50°F
Zone 2   −50° to −40°
Zone 3   −40° to −30°
Zone 4   −30° to −20°
Zone 5   −20° to −10°
Zone 6   −10° to 0°
Zone 7   0° to 10°
Zone 8   10° to 20°
Zone 9   20° to 30°
Zone 10   30° to 40°

Glossary

ACID SOIL. See pH.

ALKALINE SOIL. See pH.

ANALOGOUS COLOR HARMONY. A planting made up of three colors that appear in a row on the color wheel.

ANNUAL. A plant that is sown, flowers, sets seeds, and dies all within one season.

BACILLUS POPILLIA. Milky spore disease, a bacteria that infects Japanese beetles.

BACILLUS THURINGIENSIS. A bacteria that infects such susceptible insect pests as cabbage looper, gypsy moth, and bagworm.

BARE-ROOTED PLANT. A plant without soil attached to its roots.

BED. Flower beds are plantings, such as those in the middle of a yard, that are accessible from all sides and intended to be viewed from all sides.

BIENNIAL. A plant that takes two years to complete its growing cycle from seed; usually flowers, fruits, and dies during its second season.

BORDEAUX MIXTURE. A fungicide made by combining copper sulfate, lime, and water.

BORDER. Flower borders are plantings along the edge of an area such as a fence, driveway, or foundation, usually accessible and viewed from only one side.

BULB. The fleshy root of plants such as some iris; the bulb stores the roots, stems, leaves, and flowers for the next season's growth.

CLAY SOIL. A soil containing from thirty- to 100-percent clay; fine-textured and sticky when wet.

COLOR HARMONY. Color scheme.

COMPLEMENTARY COLOR HARMONY. A planting made up of two colors that are directly opposite one another on the color wheel.

COMPOST. A rich, porous soil of completely decayed organic matter.

CONTACT INSECTICIDE. A formulation that kills upon contact with some external portion of the insect's body.

COTYLEDON. The seed, or first, leaves of a germinating plant.

CROWN. The area of a seed plant where the root and stem merge.

CULTIVAR. A cultivated variety, usually unique and an improvement in the species, created by the successful cross-pollination of two different plants within a species.

DAMPING OFF. A fungus disease carried in unsterile soil that causes young seedlings to wither and die.

DEADHEADING. Cutting off flower heads after they bloom.

DECIDUOUS PLANT. A plant that sheds most or all of its leaves yearly; not evergreen.

DISBUDDING. Removing most buds from a developing plant in order to leave one bud of increased size and strength.

DIVISION. A method of plant propagation in which plants (including their root systems) are dug and cut apart; the resulting plants can all be replanted.

DRIFT. A large, informally shaped group of plants of the same species.

EVERGREEN. A plant whose foliage stays green and functional through more than one growing season.

EXTENSION SERVICE. This agency is the educational arm of the U.S. Federal Department of Agriculture. There is a branch in every county in the country, often affiliated with the state university.

FLAT. A shallow, topless box with drainage slits or holes in the bottom, used for sowing seeds, inserting cuttings, and transplanting young seedlings.

FUMIGANT. A chemical that produces a killing vapor in the air.

FUNGICIDE. A formulation that destroys or inhibits the growth of fungi.

GERMINATION. The sprouting of seeds.

GRANDIFLORA. A plant that contains both single blooms and clusters of blooms.

GROUND COVER. Low-growing plants that cover the ground instead of lawn grass.

HARDINESS ZONES. U.S. Department of Agriculture classifications according to annual minimum temperatures and/or lengths of growing seasons. See zone map, page 142.

HUMUS. The resultant brown substance that develops following the breakdown of organic materials by various soil organisms.

HYBRID. A new plant created by the successful cross-pollination of two plants of two different species, thus with different genetictraits.

INSECTICIDAL SOAP. A specially prepared, biodegradable soap made from natural fatty substances that kills many insects on contact without damaging plants or harming people, animals, or beneficial insects.

INSECTICIDE. A formulation that destroys insects.

LEAF MOLD. Partially decayed leaves.

LIFT. To take a plant up out of the place where it is growing.

LOAM. A soil consisting of about a 50-50 mixture of sand and clay; a ball of damp loam will not break when handled.

MONOCHROMATIC COLOR HARMONY. A planting consisting of different shades of a single color.

MULCH. A protective covering, such as bark chips or sawdust, spread over the ground to reduce evaporation, maintain an even soil temperature, prevent erosion, control weeds, and enrich the soil.

MULTIFLORA. A plant containing clusters of flowers.

NATURALIZE. Permanently plant and leave undisturbed to spread at will.

NITROGEN. One of the three most important plant nutrients, an essential element of chlorophyll; stunted growth and pale yellow foliage indicate nitrogen deficiency. See also Potassium, Phosphorus.

NPK. Numbers representing the proportion of nitrogen, phosphorus, and potassium, respectively, in chemical fertilizers.

OFFSET. A young plant that springs up on the side of the parent plant, from where it can be easily detached and transplanted.

PEAT MOSS. Compacted plant debris, including sphagnum moss.

PERENNIAL. A plant with a life cycle of three or more seasons.

PESTICIDE. An all-embracing term for any agent that is used to destroy pests.

pH. The relative acidity and alkalinity of a soil on a scale of 1 to 14; a soil with a pH of 7 is considered neutral.

PHOSPHORUS. One of the three most important plant nutrients, essential for good root and stem development; stunted growth and purple coloring of leaves and stems indicate phosphorus deficiency. See also Nitrogen, Potassium.

PINCHING BACK. The technique of pinching out the growing point of developing plants in order to encourage bushiness.

PIP. Individual rootstock of lily-of-the-valley.

POTASSIUM. One of the three most important plant nutrients; slow growth, high incidence of disease, and bronzing of leaves indicate potassium deficiency. See also Nitrogen, Phosphorus.

PROPAGATION. A way of multiplying plants.

REPELLENT. A substance that is distasteful or malodorous enough to keep insects away.

RESIDUAL-CONTACT INSECTICIDE. A formulation sprayed or dusted onto plants that kills insects by foot contact for long periods after application.

RHIZOME. An underground, horizontal stem or root stock.

ROOTSTOCK. A root or piece of a root.

ROTOTILL. To operate a rotary tiller.

SANDY SOIL. A soil with from fifty- to 100-percent fine sands, as well as coarse sands with thirty-five- to 100-percent fine gravel and some fine sand. Although sandy soil can be formed into a ball when wet, the ball will break easily when touched.

SEEDLING. A young plant grown from seed.

SET OUT. Plant.

SOIL AMENDMENTS. Ingredients such as sand, peat moss, or compost that are added to soil to improve its texture.

SOIL TEST. A measurement of the nitrogen/phosphorus/potassium and pH levels of the soil. Gardeners can test their own soil with soil testing kits, or send soil samples to Extension Services.

SPECIES. The basic division of the living world, consisting of distinct and similar individuals that can breed together to produce offspring similar to themselves.

STOMACH POISON. An insecticide that attacks the internal organs after it has been swallowed.

SUPERPHOSPHATE. A soluble mixture of phosphates used as a fertilizer; made by treating insoluble phosphates with sulfuric acid.

SYSTEMIC INSECTICIDE. A stomach poison that is absorbed into the sap of the plants.

TENDER PERENNIAL. A perennial plant that cannot survive cold winters and therefore must be treated like an annual plant in order to grow them in certain areas.

TILLING. Working the soil by cultivating or digging it.

TOPDRESSING. A rich mixture of soil and organic matter to scatter as fertilizer over the surface of the earth.

TOPSOIL. The surface layer of soil, consisting of good loam and organic matter.

TRACE ELEMENTS. Elements, such as boron, chlorine, copper, iron, magnesium, manganese, molybdenum, and zinc, that are naturally present in healthy soil and necessary in very small amounts for plant nutrition.

TRUE LEAVES. Those leaves that appear after the cotyledons, or seed leaves.

VARIETY. A plant that is different from the true species occurring in nature.

Appendix

Society officers, addresses, and dues are subject to change.

American Fern Society
James D. Caponetti, Treasurer
Department of Botany
The University of Tennessee
Knoxville, TN 37996-1100
Dues: $10

American Hemerocallis Society
Elly Launius, Secretary
1454 Rebel Drive
Jackson, MS 39211
Dues: $12.50

American Horticultural Society
P.O. Box 0105
Mount Vernon, VA 22121
Dues: $20

American Hosta Society
Jack A. Freedman
3103 Heatherhill
Huntsville, AL 35802
Dues: $12.50

American Iris Society
Carol Ramsey
6518 Beachy Avenue
Wichita, KS 67206
Dues: $9.50

American Penstemon Society
Orville M. Steward
P.O. Box 33
Plymouth, VT 05056
Dues: $7.50

American Peony Society
250 Interlachen Road
Hopkins, MN 55343
Dues: $7.50

American Primrose Society
Brian Skidmore, Treasurer
6730 West Mercer Way
Mercer Island, WA 98040
Dues: $10

American Rock Garden Society
Buffy Parker
15 Fairmead Road
Darien, CT 06820
Dues: $15

National Chrysanthemum
   Society
Galen L. Goss
5012 Kingston Drive
Annandale, VA 22003
Dues: $8.50

MAIL-ORDER SOURCES OF PERENNIAL SEEDS

American Daylily & Perennials
P.O. Box 210
Grain Valley, MO 64029

Appalachian Nursery
Route 1, Box 275A
Honey Creek Road
Reedsville, PA 17084
Catalog, $1

Vernon Barnes & Son Nursery, Inc.
P.O. Box 250
McMinnville, TN 37110

Kurt Bluemel, Inc.
2740 Greene Lane
Baldwin, MD 21013
Catalog, $2

Bluestone Perennials
7211 Middle Ridge Road
Madison, OH 44057
Catalog, free

W. Atlee Burpee Company
300 Park Avenue at 18th Street
Warminster, PA 18974
Catalog, free

Busse Gardens
Route 2, Box 238
Cokato, MN 55321
Catalog, $2

Canyon Creek Nursery
3527 Dry Creek Road
Oroville, CA 95965
Catalog, $1

Carroll Gardens
P.O. Box 310
Westminster, MD 21157
Catalog, $2

The Country Garden
Route 2, Box 455A
Crivitz, WI 54114
Catalog, $1

Farmer Seed & Nursery Co.
Division of Plantron Inc.
Faribault, MN 55021

Henry Field Seed & Nursery
  Company
1 Meadow Ridge Road
Shenandoah, IA 51601

Fleming's Flower Fields
8106 South 14th Street
Lincoln, NE 68512
Catalog, free

Greenwood Nursery
P.O. Box 1610
Goleta, CA 93116

Gurney Seed & Nursery Corp.
Gurney Building
Yankton, SD 57079

Harris Garden Trends
961 Lyell Ave.
Rochester, NY 14606

Holbrook Farm & Nursery
Route 2, Box 223B
Fletcher, NC 28732
Catalog, $2

J.W. Jung Company
Box B281
335 South High Street
Randolph, WI 53957
Catalog, free

Klehm Nursery
Route 5, 197 Penny Road
South Barrington, IL 60010
Catalog, $2

Orol Ledden & Sons Inc.
P.O. Box 7
Center and Atlantic Avenues
Sewell, NJ 08080

Earl May Seed & Nursery
  Company
Box 500
208 North Elm Street
Shenandoah, IA 51603
Catalog, free

McConnell Nurseries, Inc.
Port Burwell, Ontario
Canada, N0J 1T0

Mellinger's, Inc.
2310 West South Range Road
North Lima, OH 44452

Mileager's Gardens
4838 Douglas Avenue
Racine, WI 53402
Catalog, $1

Nichols Garden Nursery
1190 North Pacific Highway
Albany, OR 97321

George W. Park Seed Company
P.O. Box 46
Cokesbury Road
Greenwood, SC 29648
Catalog, free

W.H. Perron Co. Ltd.
515 Labelle Boulevard
Chomedey Laval
Quebec, Canada H7V 2T3

Rocknoll Nursery
9210 U.S. 50 East
Hillsboro, OH 45133
Catalog, $.50

Schreiner's Garden Inc.
3625 Quinaby Road, N.E.
Salem, OR 97303

Spring Hill Nurseries Co., Inc.
110 West Elm Street
Tipp City, OH 45371

Stokes Seeds, Inc.
Box 548
1049 Stokes Building
Buffalo, NY 14240

Thompson and Morgan
P.O. Box 1308
Farraday and Gramme Avenues
Jackson, NJ 08527
Catalog, free

K. Van Bourgondien & Sons
Box A
245 Farmingdale Road
Babylon, NY 11702
Catalog, free

Andre Viette Farm & Nursery
Route 1, Box 16
State Route 608
Fisherville, VA 22939
Catalog, $2

Wayside Gardens
1 Garden Lane
Hodges, SC 29695
Catalog, $1

White Flower Farm
Route 63
Litchfield, CT 06759
Catalog, $5

FURTHER READING

The Complete Shade Gardener, George Schenk, Houghton Mifflin
    Company, 1984
Complete Guide to Pest Control, George W. Ware, Thomson
    Publications, 1988
Diseases and Pests of Ornamental Plants, Pascal P. Pirone, 5th edition,
    John Wiley & Sons, 1978
Gardening with Perennials, Joseph Hudak, Timber Press, 1985
Gardening by Mail 2, Barbara J. Barton, Tusker Press, 1987
Low-Maintenance Perennials, Robert S. Hebb, Quadrangle/The New
    York Times Book Company, 1975
The Perennial Garden, Jeff and Marilyn Cox, Rodale Press, 1985
Perennials, Pamela Harper and Frederick McGourty, HP Books, 1985
The Picture Book of Perennials, Arno and Irene Nehrling, Arco
    Publishing Company, 1977
Plant Portraits, Beth Chatto, David R. Godine Publisher, 1985
Rock Gardening, H. Lincoln Foster, Timber Press, 1982
Successful Gardening with Perennials, Helen VanPelt Wilson,
    Doubleday & Company, 1976
Successful Perennial Gardening, Lewis and Nancy Hill, Garden Way
    Publishing, 1988
Taylor's Guide to Perennials, Gordon P. DeWolf, Jr., editor, Houghton
    Mifflin Company, 1986

Index

We'd love your thoughts...

Your reactions, criticisms, things you did or didn't like about this Storey/Garden Way Publishing Book. Please use space below (or write a letter if you'd prefer — even send photos!) telling how you've made use of the information...how you've put it to work...the more details the better! Thanks in advance for your help in building our library of good Storey/Garden Way Publishing books.

M. John Storey
Publisher

Book Title: _____

Purchased From: _____

Comments: _____

_____

_____

_____

_____

_____

Your Name: _____

Address: _____

_____

☐ Please check here if you'd like our latest Storey/Garden Way Publishing Books for Country Living Catalog.

☐ You have my permission to quote from my comments, and use these quotations in ads, brochures, mail, and other promotions used to market your books.

Signed _____ Date _____

From: _____

BUSINESS REPLY MAIL
FIRST CLASS   PERMIT NO.2   POWNAL, VT

Postage will be paid by addressee

 STOREY

Storey Communications, Inc.
Schoolhouse Road
RD# 1 Box 105
Pownal, VT 05261—9990

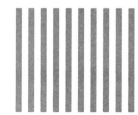